OFFICIAL
Instant Pot
BOOK

The "I LOVE MY INSTANT POT®"

Cooking for One

Recipe Book

From *Chicken and Wild Rice Soup* to *Sweet Potato Casserole with Brown Sugar Pecan Crust*, 175 Easy and Delicious Single-Serving Recipes

Lisa Childs of TriedTestedandTrue.com

Adams Media
New York London Toronto Sydney New Delhi

To Brett, Kenji, and Miya

Thank you for giving me a life more beautiful than I could ever imagine.
You are my everythings and I love you endlessly. Thank you for always
believing in me more than myself (and for doing so many dishes!).

Adams Media
An Imprint of Simon & Schuster, Inc.
100 Technology Center Drive
Stoughton, Massachusetts 02072

First Adams Media trade paperback edition
July 2021

ADAMS MEDIA and colophon are trademarks of
Simon & Schuster.

For information about special discounts for
bulk purchases, please contact Simon &
Schuster Special Sales at 1-866-506-1949 or
business@simonandschuster.com.

The Simon & Schuster Speakers Bureau can
bring authors to your live event. For more
information or to book an event contact
the Simon & Schuster Speakers Bureau at
1-866-248-3049 or visit our website at
www.simonspeakers.com.

Interior design by Michelle Kelly
Interior layout by Julia Jacintho
Photographs by James Stefiuk

Manufactured in the United States of America

10 9 8 7 6 5 4 3 2

Library of Congress
Cataloging-in-Publication Data
Names: Childs, Lisa, author.
Title: The "I love my Instant Pot®" cooking
for one recipe book / Lisa Childs of
TriedTestedandTrue.com.
Description: Stoughton, MA: Adams Media, 2021.
| Series: "I love my" series. | Includes index.
Identifiers: LCCN 2021000307 |
ISBN 9781507215777 (pb) |
ISBN 9781507215784 (ebook)
Subjects: LCSH: Smart cookers. | Pressure
cooking. | LCGFT: Cookbooks.
Classification: LCC TX840.S63 C55 2021 |
DDC 641.5/87--dc23
LC record available at
https://lccn.loc.gov/2021000307

ISBN 978-1-5072-1577-7
ISBN 978-1-5072-1578-4 (ebook)

Contents

Introduction

There are many times when a single-serving meal is just the right fit. Maybe you want to try a certain flavor or type of dish without committing to making eight servings of it. Perhaps you just need a little late-night dessert to cap off your evening. You may need to accommodate one person's dietary restriction when cooking a larger meal. Or maybe you just don't want to eat what everyone else is eating! Regardless of how many people live and eat in your home, there will always be instances where you need only a single-portion meal.

In this book, you'll find 175 comforting, healthy, and generous single-serving recipes that use your Instant Pot®, the time-saving device that allows you to cook a meal and still enjoy life! This multifunction cooking tool allows you to sauté, brown, steam, and warm your food. It cooks soups, eggs, and even cheesecakes! And the high-pressure cooking and steaming ability of an Instant Pot® does wonders for beef, pork shoulders, and chicken. With the touch of a button, you'll find that cuts of meat that normally take hours to cook can be finished in just minutes. The Instant Pot® cooks at a high temperature due to the high pressure within the pot. It also has a slow cook feature, which can replace a slow cooker in your kitchen. This cooking method also seals in essential vitamins and minerals and allows the Instant Pot® to turn out healthier, better-tasting food that is perfect when you're on the go.

Whether you've just bought your Instant Pot® or have been using it for years and just need some inspiration, this book is for you. Try cooking a new recipe (or two or three!) each week. You'll quickly learn how easy it is to integrate this multifunctional machine into every meal and snack of the day—from dishes like Blueberry Cream Cheese French Toast Bake and Herby Chicken Noodle Soup to Fall-Apart Beef Short Ribs and Gravy and Molten Chocolate Lava Cake.

With your Instant Pot®, you'll save money and time, plus you'll be able to treat yourself to beautiful and affordable meals at home—no more drive-through meals or cereal for supper! Even if you are cooking just for yourself, you deserve to eat healthy, hearty, and delicious meals. Using the tips and recipes in this book, you will gain the confidence and skills necessary to successfully and deliciously cook for one.

Instant Pot® Cooking for One

In this chapter, you will learn how to use and truly understand cooking with an Instant Pot®. Many of the technical points are well explained in the appliance's user manual, which I encourage you to read. This chapter will also teach you tips and analogies that'll give you the confidence to use your Instant Pot® every day.

Instant Pot® 101— What You Should Know

The Instant Pot® is an electric pressure cooker. Pressure cookers boil small amounts of liquid such as water or broth to create steam that gets locked into the pot and increases the cooking temperature—it's a technique that is difficult to replicate in traditional preparation methods. With nowhere to go, the steam forces itself into the food, which is why foods are able to cook so quickly. Here are some other important Instant Pot® facts you'll need to know:

- Everything you make in the Instant Pot® cooks in a wet environment and requires liquid to cook. The appliance does not bake, toast, or fry. Nothing you make in the Instant Pot® will come out crispy or browned on its own.
- The most important step in using an Instant Pot® is closing the knob. The knob must be in the Sealed position to ensure the steam and pressure stays locked inside the pot. When removing the pot, the knob must be in the Venting position.
- The Instant Pot® will display numbers counting *down* from the cook time you've set. Once the pressure cooking is completed, the display will read "L0:00" and start counting *up*, letting you know how many minutes it has been naturally releasing the pressure. "L" stands for "lapsed time."

Instant Pot® Buttons

The Instant Pot® has many different function buttons that can be intimidating and confusing. No need to fret. All of these buttons are simply presets that can be adjusted manually. Most people will only use the following buttons:

Manual/Pressure Cook Button

Think of this as the "time cook" button on your microwave. The pot will default to high pressure, and you'll adjust the number of minutes using the +/- buttons.

Sauté Button

This is one of the genius features of the Instant Pot®—you can sauté right in the pot! Unlike a slow cooker, which requires you to precook or sear foods on the stove, the Instant Pot® turns into a stovetop when you use the Sauté function. Pressing the Sauté button multiple times will also adjust the temperature from Low to High to a Custom setting. You'll notice that a small handful of recipes in this book use only the Sauté button—no pressure cooking required. These recipes cook quickly or require a minimal amount of liquid, but they still benefit from using the Instant Pot® as a convenient cooktop (for example, Savory Biscuits and Gravy in Chapter 2, Korean Sautéed Spinach in Chapter 4, and Brown Butter–Cinnamon Rice Crispy Treat in Chapter 11).

Yogurt Button

All but a couple of models of Instant Pot® come with a Yogurt button, meaning the pot will warm up very slowly and mildly, creating the perfect environment to incubate yogurt. However, you can also use the Yogurt button to quickly proof bread dough, as it sets the ideal temperature for yeast to thrive.

Natural Pressure Release (NPR) versus Quick Pressure Release (QR)

In Instant Pot® recipes, you'll see instructions for either a quick release, full natural pressure release, or a natural pressure release for a certain number of minutes, followed by a quick release. These options are given because the pressure must be completely released from the pot before the lid will unlock to be opened. Different foods will take different amounts of time to cook at full pressure followed by a time at lower pressure.

It's just like cooking a prime rib in the oven—you'll cook at a high temperature first, then turn off the oven and let it continue to cook using residual heat. The Instant Pot® is still cooking with residual heat during a natural pressure release, so it's important to note which foods you'll want to release quickly.

I like to explain the difference between the different releases with a soda bottle analogy. Imagine taking a soda bottle and shaking it up to create a lot of pressure in the bottle.

A *quick pressure release* would be like taking the cap off the bottle quickly and releasing all that pressure in one go. In the Instant Pot®, this method is used for foods that need to stop cooking quickly or that do not require a lower-pressure environment to finish the second half of the cooking process.

A *full natural pressure release* is like cracking the soda bottlecap just a little bit to slowly release the built-up pressure in the bottle.

A *natural pressure release for X amount of minutes* is like cracking the lid to let a little pressure out for the prescribed number of minutes, then taking the cap off completely.

All Instant Pot® recipes will require one of these three pressure-release methods.

Instant Pot® Accessories

When asked about what accessories to buy for the Instant Pot®, I always tell people to buy nothing. Yes, that's right. Learn how to use your Instant Pot® first, and that'll tell you what kind of accessories you'll need and want based on the food you like to cook. That being said, these are the accessories I have used and find useful specifically when cooking recipes for one.

Steamer Basket

I use a steamer basket all the time to steam vegetables, lift out squash, or make bone broth. This is the number one accessory that most people use in their pots.

Trivet

A trivet, or small round rack, comes with your Instant Pot® and is a frequently used tool while pressure cooking. Do not toss it, as it'll be used to keep foods out of the cooking liquid.

6" Cake Pan

This pan is used in almost all of my pot-in-pot recipes, such as the Blueberry Cream Cheese French Toast Bake (see Chapter 2), Cheesy Cajun Shrimp and Grits (see Chapter 8), Teriyaki-Glazed Meatloaf and Mashed Potatoes (see Chapter 6), and many desserts (see Chapter 11). This pan is perfect to use for single-serving cooking because it is pressure safe and perfectly portioned.

Silicone Egg Bites Mold

Normally I don't recommend this accessory, because it makes such small portions that it's a little impractical when cooking for larger families. However, this is an awesome tool when cooking for one. Use it to make Small-Batch Bacon-Cheddar Egg Bites (see Chapter 2) or Crustless Pumpkin Pie Bites and Small-Batch Cherry Cheesecake Bites (see both in Chapter 11).

8-Ounce Ramekin

Many breakfast egg dishes, dips, and desserts are made in a ceramic pressure-proof ramekin. This is the perfect single-serving size.

$\frac{1}{8}$ Teaspoon Measuring Spoon

This is not a standard-sized measuring spoon that you'll find with most sets, but I use it daily. It's acceptable to estimate half of a ¼ teaspoon, but having this measuring spoon is extremely helpful when creating single-portion meals that use smaller quantities of spices.

Cleaning Your Instant Pot®

You can find a free guide on how to clean your Instant Pot® on my website, TriedTestedandTrue.com, as well as a *YouTube* video (www.youtube.com/watch?v=dZgACiivovs) showing you all the parts and how to clean them. Here are my top cleaning tips:

- Use a damp paper towel to wipe down the outside of the pot.
- The inner pot and sealing rings are dishwasher safe.
- The lid has several parts and inner crevices that can retain water. For this reason, I take apart the components and wash the lid by hand.
- Store the Instant Pot® with the lid upside down on the base to help odors dissipate and prevent them from getting locked in your pot.

The 3- versus 6-Quart Instant Pot®

You may believe that a 3-quart Instant Pot® is best for cooking for one, but it's not necessarily the case. A 3-quart will work for almost every recipe in this book, but I find it too small if cooking more than a single portion. A steamer basket does not fit inside a 3-quart pot, and you may not be able to cook in bulk (which you'll want to do if you like to meal prep for several recipes at once). I like to use my 3-quart pot to make side dishes while I make the main meal in my 6-quart pot. A 6-quart will be able to fit things like crab legs, multiple ramekins, and larger pot-in-pot vessels. Most recipes you'll find on the Internet are developed for a 6-quart Instant Pot®. However, apart from the size, there is no difference between the 3-quart and the 6-quart Instant Pot®, and both are fantastic.

First-Time Use

After you take your Instant Pot® out of the box and clean it, you'll want to run a water test to ensure the pot functions correctly. This test simply pressure cooks water to make sure the pot comes to pressure. It also helps you get accustomed to using the buttons. Here is how to do it:

1. Ensure all the parts are put together, the machine is plugged in, and the sealing ring is snug in the lid.
2. Add 2 cups water to the inner pot and close the lid.
3. Turn the knob to Sealing. If your model does this automatically, then move on to the next step.

4. Press the Pressure Cook or Manual button and use the + button to adjust to 5 minutes. After a couple of seconds, the Instant Pot® will beep and the display will say "ON." This means it has understood the command and is beginning to pressurize.
5. While the pot is pressurizing, some steam will come out of the knob, and the pin may start rattling. This is normal and expected, as the water is starting to boil and the steam is moving the pin. When the pin pops up and is flush with the lid, there should be no steam escaping from the lid; the pot is fully pressurized and will start counting down from 5.
6. When the display reads "L0:00," the pot will automatically begin to slowly depressurize, also known as natural pressure release. Releasing the pressure at 0 is called a quick pressure release.
7. Turn the knob from Sealing to Venting, being careful not to put your hand or face over the vent. The steam and pressure will come out of the lid quickly at first, then fade as it depressurizes. When the pin falls down, you'll know it's time to open the lid. The lid will not open while pressurized, so do not try to wiggle the lid or press the pin down to pry the lid off.
8. Twist the lid off and celebrate! You successfully used your Instant Pot® and it was probably a lot less stressful than you imagined! Now, clean the pot and lid with soap and water, and you're ready to cook with the Instant Pot®.

Cooking for One: Tips and Hacks

Cooking a single portion or any amount for one person may feel daunting at first, but with these tips, you'll feel much more confident knowing you can enjoy beautiful, delicious meals at home in smaller quantities.

- **Plan your meals around the largest ingredient you have.** For example, if you buy a large package of chicken breasts or a big bag of produce, look for multiple recipes in this book that use that ingredient.

- **Freeze ingredients that you may not use right away but like to have on hand,** such as cheese, vegetables, fruit, bread, and protein. I like to immediately portion out ground meat in ¼-cup or ¼-pound portions and freeze. That way, I can quickly grab the amount I need to cook a meal for one.

- **Use dried onion flakes in place of fresh onion.** In recipes for one, you'll usually only use about ¼ of a whole onion, which leads to a lot of waste. Instead, purchase a large container of dehydrated onion flakes (in the spice aisle) and use about a tablespoon in recipes. That way, you'll always have it on hand, never need to worry about wasting it, and your hands never smell of onion.

- **Use frozen versus canned foods.** In many recipes, you only need to use a small portion of a whole can, which may lead to waste. Frozen foods taste fresher, and you can take out the portion you need and keep the rest in the freezer.

- **Think outside the box.** You can find smaller portions of many foods and ingredients in many unexpected places. When you get takeout, save up the individual-sized packets of spices and sauces. Most grocery stores have precut and packaged produce, marinated meats, and fresh pastas in smaller portions. A leftover vegetable tray can easily be chopped up for tomorrow's soup.

- **Use jarred or tubed garlic.** Many of the recipes in this book use garlic. Instead of using a tiny bit of a whole clove of fresh garlic, I always have a jar of minced garlic in my refrigerator. It keeps forever and has a superior flavor to garlic powder. If you use garlic sparingly but still like it fresh, I recommend using the tubes of freshly grated garlic sold in the fresh herb aisle.

- **Get to know your grocery store.** You may be surprised to learn that your butcher or the bakery may package you a smaller portion than what's on the shelf if you kindly ask! My grocery store also has a number of buffet-style salad bars where I can pick up smaller portions of vegetables, meats, condiments, olives, sauces, fruits, breads, and seeds. This is a great option if you only need a small portion for a recipe and don't want to purchase a whole package.

- **Use bouillon paste.** I always have a jar of Better Than Bouillon Roasted Chicken Base in my refrigerator. Not only does it add wonderful flavor; it also easily mixes with water to make chicken broth in minutes in any quantity I need. This is a much better alternative to purchasing cans or boxes of broth that will need to be used up within days of opening.

- **Shop at the Dollar Store.** At the Dollar Store you can find some small food packages and cans of products not sold at regular stores, such as mini cans of sweetened condensed milk, flour, spices, sauces, and noodles. These are excellent products for single-portion cooking.

I hope that by using the knowledge and tips in this chapter, you can go forth and start cooking with confidence in your Instant Pot®! I recommend picking a handful of recipes that sound good to you and start there. All of the step-by-step recipes in this book are easy to make and have been tested for success. Good luck!

2

Breakfast for One

Breakfast is a versatile meal in our culture, where both an egg white omelet and powdered sugar doughnut are perfectly acceptable as the first meal of the day. This chapter offers a diverse menu of breakfast options for everyone, both sweet and savory recipes.

If you're ever short on time in the morning, try one of the oatmeal recipes that can be thrown in the Instant Pot® first thing and served when you're ready. No babysitting and standing over a stove required! If you need breakfast ready to go, definitely make the Instant Pot® Single-Serving Vanilla Bean Yogurt or Two-Layered Creamy Pumpkin Yogurt. Also, any of the egg dishes may be made ahead and reheated in the microwave.

When you have just a little bit more time to spare, the Small-Batch Bacon-Cheddar Egg Bites are an affordable and delicious restaurant copy-cat. And even kids will love the Maple Sausage Pancake Bites—they'll be gone in minutes!

You're sure to love all these delicious, healthy, indulgent, and simple breakfast recipes for one!

Cheesy Breakfast Ham and Hash

The classic flavors of ham, Cheddar, potatoes, and eggs combine into a single-serving ramekin that can be whipped up while you get ready for your day, and enjoyed in one sitting that'll fill you up until lunch.

- **Hands-On Time: 3 minutes**
- **Cook Time: 25 minutes**

Serves 1

2 large eggs
½ tablespoon butter, melted
¼ cup frozen hash browns or potatoes
2 tablespoons diced ham
½ tablespoon chopped pickled jalapeño peppers
2 tablespoons shredded Cheddar cheese
⅛ teaspoon salt
1 cup water
1 tablespoon salsa

1 Grease an 8-ounce ramekin. Set aside.

2 In a small bowl, whisk together eggs and butter. Add potatoes, ham, jalapeños, Cheddar, and salt. Combine completely.

3 Pour mixture into prepared ramekin and cover with foil.

4 Pour water into Instant Pot® and add the trivet. Place ramekin on trivet.

5 Close the lid; turn the knob to Sealing.

6 Press Manual or Pressure Cook button and adjust time to 20 minutes.

7 When the timer beeps, allow 5 minutes to naturally release the pressure, then remove the lid.

8 Carefully remove ramekin from the Instant Pot® and remove foil. Serve topped with salsa.

PER SERVING

CALORIES: 325 | FAT: 20g | PROTEIN: 21g | SODIUM: 933mg
FIBER: 1g | CARBOHYDRATES: 11g | SUGAR: 1g

Green Chili–Cheddar Egg Puff

This breakfast casserole has been scaled down to be easier to make any day. If you've indulged in a personal Vanilla Bean Crème Brûlée or Gooey Chocolate Chip Cookie Sundae (see recipes in Chapter 11) and have extra egg whites, try substituting 3–4 egg whites in place of the 2 whole eggs in this recipe.

- **Hands-On Time: 5 minutes**
- **Cook Time: 20 minutes**

Serves 1

2 large eggs
½ tablespoon butter, melted
2 tablespoons cottage cheese
1 tablespoon chopped green chilies
2 tablespoons shredded Cheddar cheese
½ tablespoon all-purpose flour
⅛ teaspoon salt
1⁄16 teaspoon ground black pepper
1⁄16 teaspoon garlic powder
1⁄16 teaspoon ground cayenne pepper
1 cup water

1 Grease an 8-ounce ramekin. Set aside.

2 In a small bowl, whisk together eggs and butter. Add cottage cheese, chilies, Cheddar, flour, salt, black pepper, garlic powder, and cayenne pepper. Combine completely.

3 Pour mixture into prepared ramekin and cover with foil.

4 Pour water into Instant Pot® and add the trivet. Place ramekin on trivet.

5 Close the lid; turn the knob to Sealing.

6 Press Manual or Pressure Cook button and adjust time to 15 minutes.

7 When the timer beeps, allow 5 minutes to naturally release the pressure, then remove the lid.

8 Carefully remove ramekin from Instant Pot® and remove foil. Serve immediately.

PER SERVING

CALORIES: 295 | FAT: 19g | PROTEIN: 20g | SODIUM: 673mg
FIBER: 1g | CARBOHYDRATES: 6g | SUGAR: 2g

Sourdough Avocado Toast with Soft-Boiled Egg

When you're making a single slice of avocado toast and need only a single soft-boiled egg, the Instant Pot® is the perfect tool for the job! Soft-boiled eggs don't store well, so they must be made fresh. Instead of going through all the hassle of cooking one egg on the stove, just place it in the Instant Pot®, and it'll be done in minutes!

- **Hands-On Time: 5 minutes**
- **Cook Time: 5 minutes**

Serves 1

1 cup water

1 large egg

½ medium avocado, peeled, pitted, and sliced

1 (1-ounce) slice sourdough bread, toasted

⅛ teaspoon salt

⅛ teaspoon ground black pepper

⅛ teaspoon crushed red pepper flakes

½ tablespoon roasted pepitas

½ teaspoon olive oil

1 Pour water into Instant Pot® and add the trivet. Place egg on trivet.

2 Close the lid; turn the knob to Sealing.

3 Press Manual or Pressure Cook button and adjust time to 5 minutes.

4 When the timer beeps, immediately turn the knob from Sealing to Venting, then remove the lid and carefully transfer egg to an ice bath while assembling toast.

5 Spread avocado slices evenly over toast. Carefully peel soft-boiled egg and place it on top of avocado.

6 Sprinkle salt, black pepper, red pepper flakes, pepitas, and oil over avocado. Break open egg with fork and serve immediately.

PER SERVING

CALORIES: 302 | FAT: 18g | PROTEIN: 12g | SODIUM: 536mg
FIBER: 6g | CARBOHYDRATES: 22g | SUGAR: 2g

Mediterranean Feta Frittata

This super-savory breakfast dish is light, healthy, and sure to start your day off beautifully. To boost your vegetable intake, try adding some chopped tomatoes, bell peppers, or mushrooms to this dish. And don't forget the balsamic glaze—it really takes this frittata to the next level!

- **Hands-On Time: 3 minutes**
- **Cook Time: 15 minutes**

Serves 1

2 large eggs
½ tablespoon heavy cream
2 tablespoons chopped spinach
2 tablespoons crumbled feta cheese
½ tablespoon chopped kalamata olives
1 cup water
¼ teaspoon balsamic glaze
⅛ teaspoon salt

1 Grease an 8-ounce ramekin. Set aside.

2 In a small bowl, whisk together eggs and cream. Add spinach, feta, and olives. Combine completely.

3 Pour mixture into prepared ramekin and cover with foil.

4 Pour water into Instant Pot® and add the trivet. Place ramekin on trivet.

5 Close the lid; turn the knob to Sealing.

6 Press Manual or Pressure Cook button and adjust time to 10 minutes.

7 When the timer beeps, allow 5 minutes to naturally release the pressure, then remove the lid.

8 Carefully remove ramekin from Instant Pot® and remove foil. Drizzle with balsamic glaze and salt. Serve immediately.

PER SERVING

CALORIES: 234 | FAT: 17g | PROTEIN: 15g | SODIUM: 737mg
FIBER: 0g | CARBOHYDRATES: 2g | SUGAR: 1g

Small-Batch Bacon-Cheddar Egg Bites

Popularized by Starbucks, Sous Vide Egg Bites have become a trendy breakfast or brunch staple to enjoy with your warm morning beverage. Making them at home in the Instant Pot® will save you a lot of money, and you can enjoy them for breakfast or as a high-protein snack.

- Hands-On Time: 5 minutes
- Cook Time: 18 minutes

Serves 1

5 large eggs
¼ cup cottage cheese
⅛ teaspoon salt
1 tablespoon butter, melted
7 teaspoons crumbled bacon bits
7 tablespoons shredded Cheddar cheese
1 cup water

1 In a blender, combine eggs, cottage cheese, salt, and butter, and blend until smooth.

2 Spray a silicone egg bites mold with cooking spray. Into each cup of the mold, add 1 teaspoon bacon bits. Pour egg mixture into the mold, dividing mixture evenly among cups. Top each egg bite with 1 tablespoon Cheddar, then cover the mold with foil.

3 Pour water into Instant Pot® and add the trivet. Place mold on trivet.

4 Close the lid; turn the knob to Sealing.

5 Press Manual or Pressure Cook button and adjust time to 8 minutes.

6 When the timer beeps, allow 10 minutes to naturally release the pressure, then remove the lid.

7 Carefully remove mold from the Instant Pot® and remove foil. Invert mold onto a plate and squeeze egg bites out. Serve immediately.

PER SERVING (FULL RECIPE)

CALORIES: 783 | FAT: 53g | PROTEIN: 57g | SODIUM: 1,541mg
FIBER: 0g | CARBOHYDRATES: 4g | SUGAR: 3g

Maple-Vanilla Steel-Cut Oats

Steel-cut oats take a bit longer to cook than rolled oats, but they make a very hearty and filling breakfast. Top this simple, healthy breakfast with any sweetener or milk of your choice.

- **Hands-On Time: 3 minutes**
- **Cook Time: 25 minutes**

Serves 1

⅓ cup steel-cut oats
1 cup water
3 tablespoons maple syrup
3 tablespoons vanilla
    almond milk

1 In the Instant Pot®, combine oats and water.

2 Close the lid; turn the knob to Sealing.

3 Press Manual or Pressure Cook button and adjust time to 15 minutes.

4 When the timer beeps, allow 10 minutes to naturally release the pressure, then remove the lid.

5 Stir oats and add maple syrup and almond milk. Ladle into a bowl and serve immediately.

PER SERVING

CALORIES: 399 | **FAT:** 4g | **PROTEIN:** 10g | **SODIUM:** 35mg
FIBER: 7g | **CARBOHYDRATES:** 82g | **SUGAR:** 39g

Brown Sugar Breakfast Quinoa

If you've only used quinoa in a couple of recipes, try this superfood in a totally different way. Reminiscent of oatmeal, this sweet breakfast quinoa is an amazing way to pack your day with nutrients.

- **Hands-On Time: 5 minutes**
- **Cook Time: 12 minutes**

Serves 1

½ cup uncooked quinoa,
    rinsed
1 cup vanilla almond milk
1 tablespoon butter
1/16 teaspoon salt
2 tablespoons brown sugar
½ cup whole milk
¼ cup heavy cream

1 To the Instant Pot®, add quinoa, almond milk, butter, and salt.

2 Close the lid; turn the knob to Sealing.

3 Press Manual or Pressure Cook button and adjust time to 2 minutes.

4 When the timer beeps, allow 10 minutes to naturally release the pressure, then remove the lid.

5 Stir in brown sugar and milk and scoop into a bowl. Serve topped with cream.

PER SERVING

CALORIES: 887 | **FAT:** 42g | **PROTEIN:** 18g | **SODIUM:** 382mg
FIBER: 7g | **CARBOHYDRATES:** 105g | **SUGAR:** 50g

Creamy Instant Pot® Oatmeal

The best part about making oatmeal in the Instant Pot® is that there's no risk of it boiling over onto the stove or in the microwave. It's a "set it and forget it" type of dish.

- **Hands-On Time: 5 minutes**
- **Cook Time: 2 minutes**

Serves 1

½ cup rolled oats
1 cup water
¹⁄₁₆ teaspoon salt
½ tablespoon butter
3 teaspoons brown sugar
⅛ teaspoon vanilla extract
⅛ teaspoon ground cinnamon
½ tablespoon heavy cream

1 In the Instant Pot®, combine oats, water, and salt.

2 Close the lid; turn the knob to Sealing.

3 Press Manual or Pressure Cook button and adjust time to 2 minutes.

4 When the timer beeps, immediately turn the knob from Sealing to Venting. Remove the lid.

5 Stir oats, then add butter, brown sugar, vanilla, cinnamon, and cream. Scoop into a bowl and serve immediately.

PER SERVING

CALORIES: 278 | FAT: 11g | PROTEIN: 5g | SODIUM: 150mg
FIBER: 4g | CARBOHYDRATES: 41g | SUGAR: 14g

Toasted Coconut Oatmeal

This oatmeal recipe tastes and feels very light, but it keeps you filled up all morning. Try adding some fresh pineapple or mango chunks on top for a totally different flavor.

- **Hands-On Time: 5 minutes**
- **Cook Time: 2 minutes**

Serves 1

½ cup rolled oats
1 cup water
¹⁄₁₆ teaspoon salt
3 tablespoons cream of coconut
2 tablespoons whole milk
¼ cup raspberries
2 tablespoons toasted coconut

1 In the Instant Pot®, combine oats, water, and salt.

2 Close the lid; turn the knob to Sealing.

3 Press Manual or Pressure Cook button and adjust time to 2 minutes.

4 When the timer beeps, immediately turn the knob from Sealing to Venting. Remove the lid.

5 Stir oats, then add cream of coconut and milk. Scoop into a bowl and top with raspberries and toasted coconut. Serve immediately.

PER SERVING

CALORIES: 451 | FAT: 16g | PROTEIN: 8g | SODIUM: 194mg
FIBER: 7g | CARBOHYDRATES: 72g | SUGAR: 34g

Blueberry-Almond Oatmeal

Creamy oatmeal, pops of juicy blueberries, and a crunch of almonds and granola make this Blueberry-Almond Oatmeal a perfect blend of flavors and textures—a healthier spin on a bakery blueberry muffin.

- **Hands-On Time: 5 minutes**
- **Cook Time: 2 minutes**

Serves 1

½ cup rolled oats
½ cup water
½ cup vanilla almond milk
¹⁄₁₆ teaspoon salt
3 tablespoons blueberries
3 teaspoons brown sugar
⅛ teaspoon almond extract
¼ teaspoon ground cinnamon
1 tablespoon heavy cream
1 tablespoon granola
2 teaspoons sliced almonds

1 In the Instant Pot®, combine oats, water, almond milk, salt, and blueberries.

2 Close the lid; turn the knob to Sealing.

3 Press Manual or Pressure Cook button and adjust time to 2 minutes.

4 When the timer beeps, immediately turn the knob from Sealing to Venting. Remove the lid.

5 Stir oats, then add brown sugar, almond extract, and cinnamon. Stir to combine and scoop into a bowl. Top with cream, granola, and almonds. Serve immediately.

PER SERVING

CALORIES: 378 | FAT: 13g | PROTEIN: 8g | SODIUM: 229mg
FIBER: 7g | CARBOHYDRATES: 59g | SUGAR: 27g

STEEL-CUT VERSUS ROLLED OATS

Steel-cut oats absorb less liquid than rolled oats, so their texture is firmer and almost ricelike, while rolled oats absorb a lot of liquid quickly and become soft and gooey in texture. Steel-cut oats have a nutty or grainlike flavor, while rolled oats are very mild. Both are highly nutritious and excellent sources of vitamins, antioxidants, protein, and fiber.

Savory Biscuits and Gravy

Individually portioned biscuit dough can easily be found in most grocery stores, allowing you to enjoy this breakfast classic with no waste. Try baking premade biscuits in an air fryer while the gravy comes together, and you can have a gourmet breakfast in less than 15 minutes. For added protein, try topping your biscuits and gravy with two soft scrambled eggs and cheese.

- **Hands-On Time: 5 minutes**
- **Cook Time: 15 minutes**

Serves 1

1 slice uncooked thick-cut bacon, minced
¼ cup ground breakfast sausage
1 tablespoon all-purpose flour
¹⁄₁₆ teaspoon ground cayenne pepper
⅛ teaspoon salt
⅛ teaspoon ground black pepper
½ cup whole milk
2 cooked buttermilk biscuits, halved

1 On the Instant Pot®, press Sauté button and adjust to High. Add bacon and cook about 4 minutes until crispy. Using a slotted spoon, remove bacon and set aside, leaving the bacon grease in the pot.

2 Add sausage and sauté about 5 minutes until browned and cooked through. Sprinkle sausage with flour, cayenne pepper, salt, and black pepper. Mix to fully coat sausage and cook 1 minute.

3 Whisk in milk. Cook gravy, whisking continuously, about 3–5 minutes until thickened to the desired consistency.

4 Press Cancel button to turn off the heat and add bacon bits. Lay biscuit halves on a serving plate and top with sausage mixture. Serve immediately.

PER SERVING

CALORIES: 647 | FAT: 26g | PROTEIN: 21g | SODIUM: 1,884mg
FIBER: 2g | CARBOHYDRATES: 73g | SUGAR: 12g

Sweet Breakfast Grits

With their soothing texture and distinct flavor, grits are a great breakfast in the fall or winter. Either white or yellow grits work for this recipe—use what you have on hand. If you like this dish, you'll love the Cheesy Cajun Shrimp and Grits recipe (see Chapter 8).

- **Hands-On Time: 2 minutes**
- **Cook Time: 10 minutes**

Serves 1

¼ cup grits
½ cup whole milk
1½ cups water, divided
1 tablespoon butter
3 tablespoons brown sugar
2 tablespoons heavy cream

WHAT ARE GRITS?

Grits are made of ground corn and cooked like porridge. They have a smooth and slightly gritty texture and can be used in either sweet or savory dishes. Simply omit the brown sugar from this recipe for creamy unsweetened grits.

1 In a 6" cake pan, add grits, milk, and ½ cup water, and mix to combine.

2 Pour remaining 1 cup water into Instant Pot® and add the trivet. Place pan on trivet.

3 Close the lid; turn the knob to Sealing.

4 Press Manual or Pressure Cook button and adjust time to 10 minutes.

5 When the timer beeps, immediately turn the knob from Sealing to Venting, then remove the lid.

6 Carefully remove cake pan from Instant Pot® and mix in butter, brown sugar, and cream. Scoop into a bowl and serve, or enjoy immediately from the pan.

PER SERVING

CALORIES: 579 | **FAT:** 25g | **PROTEIN:** 8g | **SODIUM:** 75mg
FIBER: 2g | **CARBOHYDRATES:** 78g | **SUGAR:** 47g

Vegetable Egg White Delight

Vegetables for breakfast are severely underrated! If you're already chopping up vegetables for dinner, try chopping up a couple of extra tablespoons' worth and storing them in ramekins overnight. In the morning, add eggs or egg whites and pop the mixture in the Instant Pot® for a simple and easy breakfast without having to turn on the oven.

- **Hands-On Time: 5 minutes**
- **Cook Time: 20 minutes**

Serves 1

3 large egg whites
½ tablespoon butter, melted
2 tablespoons cottage cheese
1 tablespoon chopped and sautéed mushrooms
1 tablespoon chopped and sautéed red bell pepper
1 tablespoon chopped and sautéed yellow onion
2 tablespoons chopped and sautéed spinach
2 tablespoons shredded Cheddar cheese
½ tablespoon all-purpose flour
⅛ teaspoon salt
1/16 teaspoon ground black pepper
1/16 teaspoon garlic powder
1/16 teaspoon ground cayenne pepper
1 cup water

1 Grease an 8-ounce ramekin. Set aside.

2 In a small bowl, whisk together egg whites and butter. Add cottage cheese, mushrooms, bell pepper, onion, spinach, Cheddar, flour, salt, black pepper, garlic powder, and cayenne pepper. Combine completely.

3 Pour mixture into prepared ramekin and cover with foil.

4 Pour water into Instant Pot® and add the trivet. Place ramekin on trivet.

5 Close the lid; turn the knob to Sealing.

6 Press Manual or Pressure Cook button and adjust time to 15 minutes.

7 When the timer beeps, allow 5 minutes to naturally release the pressure, then remove the lid.

8 Carefully remove ramekin from Instant Pot® and remove foil. Serve immediately.

PER SERVING

CALORIES: 216 | FAT: 11g | PROTEIN: 18g | SODIUM: 652mg
FIBER: 1g | CARBOHYDRATES: 7g | SUGAR: 2g

Instant Pot® Single-Serving Vanilla Bean Yogurt

The beauty of making individual portions is that you can completely customize each cup of yogurt with your desired amount of sugar and flavor combinations, so breakfast is never boring. Feel free to substitute sugar or sweetener for the sweetened condensed milk, or omit it altogether for tart, plain yogurt that can be used as a sour cream substitute.

- **Hands-On Time: 2 minutes**
- **Cook Time: 6 hours**

Serves 1

¾ cup ultra-pasteurized whole milk

¼ teaspoon yogurt starter, such as store-bought plain yogurt

1 tablespoon sweetened condensed milk

¼ teaspoon vanilla extract

¼ teaspoon vanilla bean paste

1 cup water

YOGURT TIPS

- It's imperative to use ultra-pasteurized milk for this method of yogurt making.
- Ensure that your starter is completely whisked into the milk to prevent grainy yogurt.
- A longer incubation time will result in a more tart finished product.
- Using the Fairlife brand of ultra-filtered milk along with a sugar-free sweetener also results in a low-carb, high-protein option that is just as good as the original.

1 In an 8-ounce Mason jar or ramekin, mix all ingredients except water very thoroughly. Cover with plastic wrap or foil.

2 Pour water into Instant Pot® and add the trivet. Place jar on trivet.

3 Close the lid; turn the knob to Venting.

4 Press Yogurt button and adjust to Normal. Adjust time to 6 hours.

5 When the yogurt cycle has completed, the display will read "YOGT." Remove the lid and remove the jar from the Instant Pot®. Cover the jar with plastic wrap or the jar lid and then transfer to the refrigerator. Chill overnight, then serve.

PER SERVING

CALORIES: 178 | FAT: 7g | PROTEIN: 7g | SODIUM: 102mg
FIBER: 0g | CARBOHYDRATES: 20g | SUGAR: 20g

Two-Layered Creamy Pumpkin Yogurt

This recipe was inspired by a name-brand pumpkin yogurt that costs more for one serving than it does to purchase all the ingredients to make this recipe several times over. The yogurt magically separates into two distinct layers during incubation, creating a beautiful pumpkin layer on the bottom, topped with a spiced yogurt on top.

- **Hands-On Time: 2 minutes**
- **Cook Time: 6 hours**

Serves 1

¾ cup ultra-pasteurized whole milk

¼ teaspoon yogurt starter, such as store-bought plain yogurt

1 tablespoon sugar

⅛ teaspoon vanilla extract

1½ tablespoons pumpkin puree

1/16 teaspoon pumpkin pie spice

1 cup water

1 In an 8-ounce Mason jar or ramekin, mix all ingredients except water very thoroughly. Cover with plastic wrap or foil.

2 Pour water into Instant Pot® and add the trivet. Place jar on trivet.

3 Close the lid; turn the knob to Venting.

4 Press Yogurt button and adjust to Normal. Adjust time to 6 hours.

5 When the yogurt cycle has completed, the display will read "YOGT." Remove the lid and remove the jar from the Instant Pot®. Cover the jar with plastic wrap or the jar lid and then transfer to the refrigerator. Chill overnight, then serve.

PER SERVING

CALORIES: 121 | FAT: 5g | PROTEIN: 6g | SODIUM: 78mg
FIBER: 1g | CARBOHYDRATES: 11g | SUGAR: 10g

Blueberry Cream Cheese French Toast Bake

My family has enjoyed a full-sized version of this yummy French toast casserole with a cream cheese glaze for Christmas morning many times. Now you can have an individual serving of it any time of the year!

- **Hands-On Time: 10 minutes**
- **Cook Time: 35 minutes**

Serves 1

French Toast
1 large egg
¾ cup whole milk
2 tablespoons granulated sugar
¼ teaspoon vanilla extract
¼ teaspoon almond extract
4 slices stale Texas Toast bread, cubed into 1" pieces
¼ cup blueberries
¼ teaspoon ground cinnamon
½ tablespoon brown sugar
1 cup water

Cream Cheese Glaze
3 tablespoons confectioners' sugar
1½ tablespoons cream cheese, softened
⅛ teaspoon vanilla extract
¼ teaspoon whole milk

1 Grease a 6" cake pan. Set aside.

2 In a small bowl, whisk together egg, milk, granulated sugar, vanilla, and almond extract.

3 Arrange bread cubes in prepared cake pan, then pour milk mixture over the top and let soak 5 minutes. Sprinkle top with blueberries, cinnamon, and brown sugar.

4 Cover pan tightly with foil.

5 Pour water into Instant Pot® and add the trivet. Place pan on trivet.

6 Close the lid; turn the knob to Sealing.

7 Press Manual or Pressure Cook button and adjust time to 35 minutes.

8 While the French toast is pressure cooking, prepare the Cream Cheese Glaze by mixing all glaze ingredients together in a small bowl.

9 When the timer beeps, immediately turn the knob from Sealing to Venting, then remove the lid.

10 Carefully remove pan from the Instant Pot®, remove foil, and cool 5 minutes.

11 Spread glaze evenly on bread and enjoy immediately.

PER SERVING

CALORIES: 851 | FAT: 20g | PROTEIN: 25g | SODIUM: 875mg
FIBER: 5g | CARBOHYDRATES: 137g | SUGAR: 77g

Maple Sausage Pancake Bites

Inspired by a popular fast-food chain's breakfast sandwich, these bite-sized morsels have a surprise bite of sausage in the middle hugged by a tender blanket of sweet maple pancake. This is easily my family's favorite recipe in this chapter.

- **Hands-On Time: 5 minutes**
- **Cook Time: 20 minutes**

Serves 1

1 cup pancake mix
¼ cup whole milk
1½ cups water, divided
3 tablespoons maple syrup
3½ fully cooked frozen
    sausage links, split in half

**MAKE YOUR OWN
PANCAKE BITES**

We love the combination of savory sausage with sweet pancakes, but you can customize these in endless ways. Try adding chocolate chips, chopped fruit, berries, pumpkin puree, nuts, sprinkles, or chopped bacon into the pancake batter in place of the sausage.

1   Grease a silicone egg bites mold. Set aside.

2   In a small bowl, mix together pancake mix, milk, ½ cup water, and maple syrup.

3   Spoon 1½ tablespoons batter into each cup of prepared mold. Place half of a sausage link in the middle of the batter in each cup, pressing down slightly. Top each sausage link with an additional ½ tablespoon batter.

4   Cover the mold with a paper towel, then cover tightly with foil.

5   Pour remaining 1 cup water into Instant Pot® and add the trivet. Place mold on trivet.

6   Close the lid; turn the knob to Sealing.

7   Press Manual or Pressure Cook button and adjust time to 15 minutes.

8   When the timer beeps, allow 5 minutes to naturally release the pressure, then remove the lid.

9   Carefully remove mold from Instant Pot®, then invert pancake bites onto a plate. Serve immediately.

PER SERVING (FULL RECIPE)

CALORIES: 514 | **FAT:** 32g | **PROTEIN:** 23g | **SODIUM:** 1,720mg
FIBER: 0g | **CARBOHYDRATES:** 122g | **SUGAR:** 58g

Denver Omelet Bake

A classic Denver omelet has ham, red onion, green bell pepper, and Cheddar cheese. Save leftover pieces of vegetables from other dishes you're preparing and throw them in a little bag or ramekin to prepare for breakfast the next day.

- **Hands-On Time: 3 minutes**
- **Cook Time: 20 minutes**

Serves 1

2 large eggs

½ tablespoon butter, melted

2 tablespoons cottage cheese

2 tablespoons diced ham

1 tablespoon diced and sautéed red onion

1 tablespoon diced green bell pepper

2 tablespoons shredded Cheddar cheese

⅛ teaspoon salt

1 cup water

1 Grease an 8-ounce ramekin. Set aside.

2 In a small bowl, whisk together eggs and butter. Add cottage cheese, ham, onion, bell pepper, Cheddar, and salt. Combine completely.

3 Pour mixture into prepared ramekin and cover with foil.

4 Pour water into Instant Pot® and add the trivet. Place ramekin on trivet.

5 Close the lid; turn the knob to Sealing.

6 Press Manual or Pressure Cook button and adjust time to 15 minutes.

7 When the timer beeps, allow 5 minutes to naturally release the pressure, then remove the lid.

8 Carefully remove ramekin from Instant Pot® and remove foil. Serve immediately.

PER SERVING

CALORIES: 320 | **FAT:** 21g | **PROTEIN:** 23g | **SODIUM:** 867mg
FIBER: 0g | **CARBOHYDRATES:** 3g | **SUGAR:** 1g

Soups, Stews, and Chowders for One

This chapter may be one of the most valuable for anyone cooking for one. Not only is making soup incredibly easy in the Instant Pot® (hello, no babysitting!), but finding a delicious soup recipe that doesn't make twelve portions is often incredibly difficult. These hearty, flavorful, thick, and easy recipes will fill your soul with warmth and love without compromising on flavor. All of these soup recipes will fit in a large soup bowl and yield about 1½–2 cups.

I recommend starting with the Chicken and Wild Rice Soup, the Chicken and Sweet Potato Curry, or the Herby Chicken Noodle Soup. Make sure you use a quality chicken, beef, or vegetable broth in these recipes for the best flavor, and add salt and other toppings such as cheese, chips, sour cream, and chopped green onions to your taste.

Please note that the recipes in this chapter use regular broth. If sodium is a concern for you, substitute with low-sodium broth.

Loaded Baked Potato Soup

Few soups are more comforting, creamy, or universally liked than this loaded potato soup! The recipe calls for 2 cups diced potatoes, but you can easily adjust this recipe to use one large or two small potatoes, whatever you have on hand. The measurements are very forgiving, so if you have 2½ cups of potato chunks, just throw them all in.

- **Hands-On Time: 8 minutes**
- **Cook Time: 8 minutes**

Serves 1

1 slice uncooked thick-cut bacon, diced

2 cups peeled and diced russet potatoes

1 teaspoon dried onion flakes

¼ teaspoon minced garlic

⅛ teaspoon salt

⅛ teaspoon ground black pepper

½ cup chicken broth

¼ cup whole milk

¼ cup heavy cream

¼ cup sour cream

¼ cup shredded Cheddar cheese, divided

1 teaspoon chopped green onion

1 On the Instant Pot®, press Sauté button and adjust to High. Add bacon and sauté about 5 minutes until crispy. Using a slotted spoon, remove bacon and set aside, leaving bacon grease in the pot.

2 Add potatoes, onion flakes, garlic, salt, pepper, and broth. Deglaze the pot, scraping all the browned bits off the bottom of the pot. Press Cancel button to turn off the heat.

3 Close the lid; turn the knob to Sealing.

4 Press Manual or Pressure Cook button and adjust time to 3 minutes.

5 When the timer beeps, immediately turn the knob from Sealing to Venting, then remove the lid.

6 Stir in milk, heavy cream, and sour cream. Using a potato masher, mash up the potatoes slightly and stir until they reach the desired consistency. Add 3 tablespoons Cheddar and stir until melted.

7 Scoop into a bowl and top with remaining 1 tablespoon Cheddar, reserved bacon, and green onion. Serve.

PER SERVING

CALORIES: 912 | FAT: 62g | PROTEIN: 23g | SODIUM: 1,388mg FIBER: 4g | CARBOHYDRATES: 56g | SUGAR: 10g

Creamy Cheddar-Cauliflower Soup

This soup is creamy, cheesy, and smooth! Cauliflower is relatively low-carb compared with potatoes and has a slightly different flavor. Instead of purchasing a large head of cauliflower, look in your grocery store's produce department where the prepared salad kits are and look for packaged bags of precut and prepared cauliflower pieces. I found a bag that was the perfect size to make this soup and the delicious Creamy Cauliflower Puree recipe (see Chapter 4).

- Hands-On Time: 5 minutes
- Cook Time: 5 minutes

Serves 1

3 cups cauliflower florets
½ cup chicken broth
½ tablespoon dried
    onion flakes
½ teaspoon minced garlic
¼ teaspoon salt
⅛ teaspoon ground
    black pepper
⅛ teaspoon garlic salt
¼ teaspoon seasoned salt
½ cup heavy cream
3 tablespoons shredded
    Cheddar cheese

1 To the Instant Pot®, add cauliflower, broth, onion flakes, minced garlic, salt, pepper, garlic salt, and seasoned salt.

2 Close the lid; turn the knob to Sealing.

3 Press Manual or Pressure Cook button and adjust time to 5 minutes.

4 When the timer beeps, immediately turn the knob from Sealing to Venting, then remove the lid and add cream.

5 Using an immersion blender or high-powered blender, blend soup until completely smooth, about 3 minutes. Stir in Cheddar, transfer to a bowl, and serve immediately.

PER SERVING

CALORIES: 593 | FAT: 49g | PROTEIN: 15g | SODIUM: 1,944mg
FIBER: 7g | CARBOHYDRATES: 23g | SUGAR: 11g

Sausage, Sweet Potato, and Spinach Soup

Sweet, tender chunks of sweet potato marry perfectly with hearty, slightly spicy sausage. Beautiful pops of baby spinach swim through the soup for an incredibly light yet hearty bowl of warmth and goodness! Don't let the short ingredient list fool you. This soup is packed with flavor!

- **Hands-On Time: 5 minutes**
- **Cook Time: 17 minutes**

Serves 1

1 cup ground Italian sausage
1 cup diced sweet potato
1½ cups chicken broth
½ tablespoon dried
   onion flakes
½ teaspoon minced garlic
1 cup packed baby spinach

FEELING LIKE SOMETHING CREAMY?

Replace half the chicken broth with coconut milk for a dairy free option, or use 1 cup chicken broth in the soup while pressure cooking and add ½ cup heavy cream to the soup after cooking.

1 On the Instant Pot®, press Sauté button and adjust to High.

2 Add sausage to Instant Pot® and cook about 3–5 minutes until mostly cooked and crumbly. Add sweet potato, broth, onion flakes, and garlic. Scrape the bottom of the pot to remove any browned bits. Press Cancel button to turn off the heat.

3 Close the lid; turn the knob to Sealing.

4 Press Manual or Pressure Cook button and adjust time to 5 minutes.

5 When the timer beeps, allow 5 minutes to naturally release the pressure, then remove the lid.

6 Add spinach and stir about 2 minutes until wilted. Scoop into a bowl and enjoy immediately.

PER SERVING

CALORIES: 603 | **FAT:** 39g | **PROTEIN:** 24g | **SODIUM:** 2,434mg
FIBER: 5g | **CARBOHYDRATES:** 33g | **SUGAR:** 8g

Easy Hearty Beef Stew

I use frozen mixed vegetables and frozen diced potatoes in this recipe to minimize waste and make it even easier to make deliciously tender and hearty beef stew. Be sure to take the time to let the soup naturally release pressure for at least 10 minutes for super-tender meat!

- **Hands-On Time: 6 minutes**
- **Cook Time: 43 minutes**

Serves 1

1½ tablespoons olive oil
1 cup beef stew meat
¼ teaspoon smoked paprika
¼ teaspoon dried thyme
⅛ teaspoon seasoned salt
1 tablespoon tomato paste
2 teaspoons dried onion flakes
½ teaspoon minced garlic
1 cup beef broth
⅓ cup sliced mushrooms
½ cup frozen diced potatoes
½ cup frozen mixed
    vegetables

LEFTOVER TOMATO PASTE

If you're lucky, you can find tomato paste in a tube that can be easily stored in the refrigerator. Otherwise, you'll have to use a small can of the thick, concentrated paste. To reduce waste, I scoop 1 tablespoon-sized dollops of tomato paste onto wax paper and freeze completely. Then, pop them into a resealable bag, store in the freezer, and use as needed.

1 On the Instant Pot®, press Sauté button and adjust to High. Add oil and heat until shiny and hot.

2 In a small bowl, sprinkle meat with paprika, thyme, and salt; toss to coat evenly. Add meat to pot and cook about 3 minutes until browned on both sides. Do not stir while searing.

3 Add tomato paste, onion flakes, and garlic to meat, and stir to coat completely.

4 Add broth and deglaze the pot, scraping all the browned bits off the bottom of the pot. Press Cancel button to turn off the heat, and add mushrooms, potatoes, and mixed vegetables.

5 Close the lid; turn the knob to Sealing.

6 Press Manual or Pressure Cook button and adjust time to 30 minutes.

7 When the timer beeps, allow 10 minutes to naturally release the pressure, then remove the lid. Transfer to a bowl and serve immediately.

PER SERVING

CALORIES: 607 | FAT: 28g | PROTEIN: 44g | SODIUM: 1,404mg
FIBER: 9g | CARBOHYDRATES: 47g | SUGAR: 3g

Chicken and Sweet Potato Curry

You won't be able to stop eating this sweet and spicy (dairy-free!) curry that's bursting with flavor and chunks of sweet potato, tender chicken, and creamy coconut milk. Serve on its own or with a side of jasmine rice or Coconut Milk Rice (see Chapter 10).

- **Hands-On Time: 5 minutes**
- **Cook Time: 7 minutes**

Serves 1

1 tablespoon butter
½ teaspoon minced garlic
½ teaspoon grated fresh ginger
2¼ teaspoons curry powder
1 cup diced chicken breast
1 cup diced sweet potato
2 teaspoons dried onion flakes
1 (14-ounce) can unsweetened full-fat coconut milk
½ cup diced tomatoes
3 tablespoons cream of coconut
¾ teaspoon salt
2 tablespoons cashew halves

1 On the Instant Pot®, press Sauté button and adjust to High. Add butter, garlic, ginger, and curry powder. Sauté about 2 minutes until very fragrant. Add chicken, sweet potato, and onion flakes. Toss everything to coat.

2 Add coconut milk, tomatoes, cream of coconut, salt, and cashews. Press Cancel button to turn off the heat.

3 Close the lid; turn the knob to Sealing.

4 Press Manual or Pressure Cook button and adjust time to 5 minutes.

5 When the timer beeps, immediately turn the knob from Sealing to Venting, then remove the lid. Stir, transfer to a bowl, and serve.

PER SERVING

CALORIES: 1,591 | FAT: 108g | PROTEIN: 66g | SODIUM: 2,011mg
FIBER: 10g | CARBOHYDRATES: 86g | SUGAR: 40g

WHAT IS CREAM OF COCONUT?
Cream of coconut is a coconut-based sweetener, mostly used to make piña coladas. It is dairy- and alcohol-free, but is found in the mixed drink aisle by the club soda. It is a sweet coconut syrup that I love to mix into Instant Pot® yogurt or in my Dairy-Free Coconut-Rice Pudding (see Chapter 11).

Creamy Corn and Ham Chowder

This is probably the easiest soup in this chapter—you'll throw together all the ingredients with no sautéing beforehand! For the corn in this recipe, you can use fresh, frozen, or canned.

- **Hands-On Time: 2 minutes**
- **Cook Time: 5 minutes**

Serves 1

1 cup diced ham
½ cup frozen diced potatoes
½ cup corn
2 teaspoons dried onion flakes
½ teaspoon minced garlic
1 cup chicken broth
¼ cup sour cream
½ cup shredded
    Cheddar cheese

1 In the Instant Pot®, add ham, potatoes, corn, onion flakes, garlic, and broth.

2 Close the lid; turn the knob to Sealing.

3 Press Manual or Pressure Cook button and adjust time to 5 minutes.

4 When the timer beeps, immediately turn the knob from Sealing to Venting, then remove the lid. Stir in sour cream and Cheddar. Transfer to a bowl and serve immediately.

PER SERVING

CALORIES: 740 | FAT: 38g | PROTEIN: 51g | SODIUM: 3,267mg
FIBER: 3g | CARBOHYDRATES: 40g | SUGAR: 8g

Spicy Vegetable Soup

Packed with vegetables (add whatever you want or have on hand!), this hearty soup gets a spicy kick from Rotel tomatoes.

- **Hands-On Time: 2 minutes**
- **Cook Time: 4 minutes**

Serves 1

1 cup frozen diced potatoes
¾ cup sliced mushrooms
1 cup frozen mixed vegetables
½ teaspoon minced garlic
1 cup vegetable broth
¼ teaspoon dried thyme
¼ teaspoon dried parsley
⅓ cup Rotel Diced Tomatoes
    and Green Chilies
1 tablespoon tomato paste

1 To the Instant Pot®, add all ingredients. Stir.

2 Close the lid; turn the knob to Sealing.

3 Press Manual or Pressure Cook button and adjust time to 4 minutes.

4 When the timer beeps, immediately turn the knob from Sealing to Venting, then remove the lid. Transfer to a bowl and serve.

PER SERVING

CALORIES: 312 | FAT: 1g | PROTEIN: 10g | SODIUM: 1,251mg
FIBER: 10g | CARBOHYDRATES: 67g | SUGAR: 7g

Chicken and Wild Rice Soup

There are few flavor and texture combinations more comforting than cream and hearty wild rice! I use a wild rice blend to save on cost and to add more texture and variety to this soup. If you have leftover wild rice that's already cooked, add the ingredients to the Instant Pot® and cook for only 5 minutes with a quick pressure release.

- **Hands-On Time: 5 minutes**
- **Cook Time: 55 minutes**

Serves 1

½ cup diced chicken breast
½ tablespoon dried
    onion flakes
½ teaspoon minced garlic
¼ cup diced carrots
¼ cup diced celery
¼ cup diced mushrooms
¼ cup uncooked wild rice
    blend
1 cup chicken broth
¼ teaspoon salt
¼ teaspoon poultry
    seasoning
¼ teaspoon dried thyme
¼ cup heavy cream
1 tablespoon all-purpose flour

1 To the Instant Pot®, add all ingredients except cream and flour.

2 Close the lid; turn the knob to Sealing.

3 Press Manual or Pressure Cook button and adjust time to 45 minutes.

4 When the timer beeps, allow 5 minutes to naturally release the pressure, then remove the lid and turn on Sauté mode.

5 In a small bowl, whisk together cream and flour.

6 When soup comes to a boil in the pot, stir in cream mixture and cook about 3 minutes until thickened. Transfer to a bowl and serve immediately.

PER SERVING

CALORIES: 556 | FAT: 23g | PROTEIN: 36g | SODIUM: 1,621mg
FIBER: 5g | CARBOHYDRATES: 46g | SUGAR: 7g

Herby Chicken Noodle Soup (pictured)

This classic chicken noodle soup is guaranteed to be one of the best you'll ever have!

- **Hands-On Time: 2 minutes**
- **Cook Time: 10 minutes**

Serves 1

¾ cup diced chicken breast
½ cup diced carrots
½ cup diced celery
1 tablespoon dried onion flakes
½ teaspoon minced garlic
1½ cups chicken broth
½ teaspoon dried tarragon
¼ teaspoon salt
¼ teaspoon dried basil
¼ teaspoon dried oregano
¼ teaspoon dried parsley
1 bay leaf
½ cup uncooked egg noodles

1. To the Instant Pot®, add all ingredients, ensuring noodles are submerged in broth.

2. Close the lid; turn the knob to Sealing.

3. Press Manual or Pressure Cook button and adjust time to 5 minutes.

4. When the timer beeps, allow 5 minutes to naturally release the pressure, then remove the lid. Transfer to a bowl and serve.

PER SERVING

CALORIES: 447 | **FAT:** 5g | **PROTEIN:** 49g | **SODIUM:** 2,131mg
FIBER: 5g | **CARBOHYDRATES:** 45g | **SUGAR:** 9g

Creamy White Chicken Chili

Simple, spicy, and super easy! Just add all the ingredients to the Instant Pot® and you'll be ready to eat in less than 15 minutes.

- **Hands-On Time: 2 minutes**
- **Cook Time: 3 minutes**

Serves 1

½ cup diced chicken breast
1 tablespoon dried onion flakes
½ teaspoon minced garlic
1 (14-ounce) can great northern beans, drained and rinsed
1 cup chicken broth
1 tablespoon chopped green chilies
¼ teaspoon salt
¹⁄₁₆ teaspoon crushed red pepper flakes
¼ teaspoon ground cumin
1½ tablespoons sour cream
¼ cup heavy cream

1. To the Instant Pot®, add all ingredients except sour cream and heavy cream.

2. Close the lid; turn the knob to Sealing.

3. Press Manual or Pressure Cook button and adjust time to 3 minutes.

4. When the timer beeps, turn the knob from Sealing to Venting, then remove the lid.

5. Stir in sour cream and heavy cream. Transfer to a bowl and serve immediately.

PER SERVING

CALORIES: 935 | **FAT:** 27g | **PROTEIN:** 63g | **SODIUM:** 2,587mg
FIBER: 23g | **CARBOHYDRATES:** 105g | **SUGAR:** 12g

Cheesy Lasagna Soup

Lasagna is delicious, but it's also a pain to make. This soup gives you all the flavors of lasagna without the work. The cheesy topping melts into the soup and fulfills all your cheese-pull dreams.

- **Hands-On Time: 5 minutes**
- **Cook Time: 20 minutes**

Serves 1

Lasagna Soup
¼ pound ground sausage
½ tablespoon dried onion flakes
1 cup beef broth
¼ teaspoon Italian seasoning
¼ teaspoon dried oregano
2 ready-to-cook lasagna noodles, broken into pieces
1 cup marinara sauce

Topping
¼ cup cottage cheese
¼ cup shredded mozzarella cheese
1 tablespoon grated Parmesan cheese

1 On the Instant Pot®, press Sauté button and adjust to High. Add sausage and onion flakes and cook about 5 minutes until mostly browned. Add broth, Italian seasoning, and oregano. Deglaze the pot, scraping all the browned bits off the bottom of the pot. Press Cancel button to turn off the heat.

2 Scatter lasagna noodles so they are submerged in broth. Pour marinara sauce on top of noodles. Do not stir.

3 Close the lid; turn the knob to Sealing.

4 Press Manual or Pressure Cook button and adjust time to 10 minutes.

5 When the timer beeps, allow 5 minutes to naturally release the pressure, then remove the lid and scoop into a bowl.

6 In a separate small bowl, mix together Topping ingredients. Spoon mixture over hot soup, gently fold in twice, and serve.

PER SERVING

CALORIES: 687 | FAT: 27g | PROTEIN: 46g | SODIUM: 2,564mg
FIBER: 6g | CARBOHYDRATES: 52g | SUGAR: 18g

Zuppa Toscana

This is one of the most popular recipes on my website. Zuppa Toscana is an Italian sausage, potato, and kale soup in a creamy, spicy broth. It's incredibly savory and easy to adjust to your taste. To make this recipe dairy-free, omit the cream or use coconut milk in its place.

- **Hands-On Time: 5 minutes**
- **Cook Time: 20 minutes**

Serves 1

1 slice uncooked thick-cut
  bacon, diced
¼ pound ground
  Italian sausage
1 cup sliced unpeeled russet
  potatoes, in thin triangles
1 tablespoon dried onion flakes
½ teaspoon minced garlic
⅛ teaspoon crushed red
  pepper flakes
1¼ cups chicken broth
1 cup chopped kale
¼ cup heavy cream

1   On the Instant Pot®, press Sauté button and adjust to High. Add bacon and sauté about 5 minutes until crispy. Using a slotted spoon, remove bacon and set aside, leaving the bacon grease in the pot.

2   Add sausage and sauté about 5 minutes until cooked. Add potatoes, onion flakes, garlic, red pepper flakes, and broth. Press Cancel button to turn off the heat. Deglaze the pot, scraping all the browned bits off the bottom of the pot.

3   Close the lid; turn the knob to Sealing.

4   Press Manual or Pressure Cook button and adjust time to 5 minutes.

5   When the timer beeps, immediately turn the knob from Sealing to Venting, then remove the lid. Press Sauté button and adjust to High.

6   Add kale and boil about 5 minutes until kale is soft and wilted. Press Cancel button to turn off the heat. Add cream, transfer to a bowl, and serve topped with reserved bacon

PER SERVING

CALORIES: 992 | FAT: 76g | PROTEIN: 31g | SODIUM: 2,388mg
FIBER: 3g | CARBOHYDRATES: 38g | SUGAR: 7g

Chicken Pot Pie Soup

I love chicken pot pie, but not all the work it entails. With this soup, I get everything I love about chicken pot pie—tender chicken and vegetables in a warm, creamy gravy and a crumbly crust for texture—all in one comforting bowl!

- **Hands-On Time: 2 minutes**
- **Cook Time: 18 minutes**

Serves 1

¾ cup diced chicken breast
⅓ cup diced carrots
⅓ cup diced celery
¾ cup diced, peeled potatoes
1 cup chicken broth
1 teaspoon dried onion flakes
¼ teaspoon garlic salt
¼ teaspoon dried tarragon
¼ teaspoon dried thyme
¼ teaspoon dried parsley
¼ cup heavy cream
1½ tablespoons all-purpose flour
2 premade biscuits

1   To the Instant Pot®, add all ingredients except cream, flour, and biscuits.

2   Close the lid; turn the knob to Sealing.

3   Press Manual or Pressure Cook button and adjust time to 5 minutes.

4   When the timer beeps, allow 10 minutes to naturally release the pressure, then remove the lid. Press Sauté button and adjust to High.

5   In a small bowl, whisk cream and flour into a paste. When soup comes to a boil, stir cream mixture into the soup and cook about 3 minutes until thickened.

6   Ladle soup into a bowl and top with biscuits to serve.

PER SERVING

CALORIES: 790 | FAT: 27g | PROTEIN: 49g | SODIUM: 2,295mg
FIBER: 5g | CARBOHYDRATES: 70g | SUGAR: 10g

TIP

You can also use croissants, baked piecrust pieces, croutons, or baked puff pastry strips in place of biscuits as the "crust" in this recipe.

Tortellini, Spinach, and Sausage Soup

I love how easy this meal is to pull together. Top it with some Parmesan cheese and dip in crusty bread for a full meal you'll make over and over.

- **Hands-On Time: 5 minutes**
- **Cook Time: 16 minutes**

Serves 1

¼ pound ground Italian sausage

½ teaspoon minced garlic

½ teaspoon Italian seasoning

1 cup chicken broth

1 cup canned diced tomatoes in juice

½ cup uncooked cheese tortellini

½ cup packed baby spinach

HOW TO STORE LEFTOVER SPINACH

Spinach can wilt and go bad very quickly, so I ensure it is as dry as possible before putting it in the refrigerator. I also keep a paper towel in the bag to absorb any liquid, which will help prolong its shelf life. Spinach can also be frozen. Use it in any cooked recipe directly from the freezer or add a large handful of frozen spinach to a smoothie.

1 On the Instant Pot®, press Sauté button and adjust to High. Add sausage and cook about 5 minutes until browned. Press Cancel button to turn off the heat.

2 Add all remaining ingredients except spinach to the Instant Pot®. Deglaze the pot, scraping all the browned bits off the bottom of the pot.

3 Close the lid; turn the knob to Sealing.

4 Press Manual or Pressure Cook button and adjust time to 4 minutes.

5 When the timer beeps, allow 5 minutes to naturally release the pressure, then remove the lid.

6 Add spinach and stir 1–2 minutes until wilted. Transfer to a bowl and serve immediately.

PER SERVING

CALORIES: 639 | FAT: 37g | PROTEIN: 28g | SODIUM: 2,433mg
FIBER: 6g | CARBOHYDRATES: 41g | SUGAR: 8g

Corn and Chicken Egg Drop Soup

You won't believe how easy it is to make the best egg drop soup you've ever had in your life! When I don't have chicken on hand, I add tofu and it's absolutely soul warming! Since there are so few ingredients in this soup, every ingredient plays an important role. Except for replacing the chicken with tofu or omitting the protein altogether, don't skip any ingredients!

- **Hands-On Time: 8 minutes**
- **Cook Time: 4 minutes**

Serves 1

¼ cup minced chicken breast
½ tablespoon cornstarch
2 cups chicken broth
½ cup frozen corn
1 tablespoon sliced green onion
½ teaspoon minced garlic
¼ teaspoon grated fresh
    ginger
1 teaspoon soy sauce
¼ teaspoon ground
    white pepper
⅛ teaspoon crushed red
    pepper flakes
1 large egg
½ teaspoon sesame oil

GINGER TIPS

Fresh ginger is a staple in my household. I purchase a knob of fresh ginger from the store, then place it in a plastic bag and freeze the entire thing. Whenever I need to use it, I shave off the skin with a spoon or knife, then grate it (frozen) for whatever recipe I need.

1 In a small bowl, mix chicken with cornstarch and set aside.

2 To the Instant Pot®, add broth, corn, green onion, garlic, ginger, soy sauce, white pepper, and red pepper flakes. Scatter chicken into the pot.

3 Close the lid; turn the knob to Sealing.

4 Press Manual or Pressure Cook button and adjust time to 1 minute.

5 When the timer beeps, immediately turn the knob from Sealing to Venting, then remove the lid. Press Sauté button and adjust to High. Bring the soup to a boil, about 3 minutes.

6 In a separate small bowl, lightly whisk the egg. When soup comes to a boil, press Cancel button to turn off the heat, and immediately drizzle egg into the Instant Pot® in a circular pattern. Do not mix soup while drizzling.

7 After 30 seconds, gently push soup from one edge of the pot to the other to distribute the egg, then transfer to a serving bowl. Top with oil and serve.

PER SERVING

CALORIES: 280 | **FAT:** 11g | **PROTEIN:** 22g | **SODIUM:** 2,245mg
FIBER: 2g | **CARBOHYDRATES:** 22g | **SUGAR:** 4g

Tomato Soup

This Tomato Soup is healthy and comforting! I find using a blender is the best way to go when blending smaller quantities of soup. If you decide to use an immersion blender, transfer the soup to a tall and narrow container to blend.

- **Hands-On Time: 10 minutes**
- **Cook Time: 30 minutes**

Serves 1

2 tablespoons butter
¼ cup diced celery
½ cup chopped carrots
1 tablespoon dried onion flakes
¼ cup tomato paste
½ cup chicken broth
¾ cup diced tomatoes
½ tablespoon sugar
½ teaspoon minced garlic
1 teaspoon dried basil
¼ teaspoon garlic salt
1½ tablespoons heavy cream

TIP

Add a couple of tablespoons of your favorite basil pesto during the pressure cooking stage for a more pronounced basil flavor. I like buying the small containers of jarred pesto that are great for cooking for one.

1 Press Sauté button on the Instant Pot® and adjust to High. Add butter and cook about 5 minutes until browned.

2 Add celery, carrots, and onion flakes. Sauté 5 minutes, then add tomato paste and stir until all vegetables are coated. Add broth, tomatoes, sugar, garlic, basil, and garlic salt. Deglaze the pot, scraping all the browned bits off the bottom of the pot. Press Cancel button to turn off the heat.

3 Close the lid; turn the knob to Sealing.

4 Press Manual or Pressure Cook button and adjust time to 15 minutes.

5 When the timer beeps, allow 5 minutes to naturally release the pressure, then remove the lid.

6 Carefully transfer mixture to a blender and blend until smooth, about 4 minutes.

7 Add cream, transfer to a bowl, and serve.

PER SERVING

CALORIES: 460 | **FAT:** 30g | **PROTEIN:** 7g | **SODIUM:** 1,878mg
FIBER: 9g | **CARBOHYDRATES:** 41g | **SUGAR:** 25g

Broccoli-Cheddar Soup

You can use fresh or frozen broccoli for this soup, which makes it really easy to throw together. If you prefer a totally smooth soup versus having chunks of broccoli, you can cook for an additional 2 minutes.

- **Hands-On Time: 5 minutes**
- **Cook Time: 7 minutes**

Serves 1

1½ cups broccoli florets
1½ cups chicken broth
1 teaspoon dried onion flakes
½ teaspoon minced garlic
3 tablespoons minced carrot
1⁄16 teaspoon smoked paprika
⅛ teaspoon salt
½ cup heavy cream
1 tablespoon all-purpose flour
1 cup shredded
   Cheddar cheese

1 To the Instant Pot®, add all ingredients except cream, flour, and Cheddar.

2 Close the lid; turn the knob to Sealing.

3 Press Manual or Pressure Cook button and adjust time to 4 minutes.

4 When the timer beeps, immediately turn the knob from Sealing to Venting, then remove the lid. Press Sauté button and adjust to High.

5 In a small bowl, whisk cream and flour into a paste. Add it to soup, whisking about 3 minutes until thickened. Press Cancel button to turn off the heat, then slowly whisk in Cheddar. Transfer to a bowl and serve.

PER SERVING

CALORIES: 962 | FAT: 75g | PROTEIN: 36g | SODIUM: 2,491mg
FIBER: 1g | CARBOHYDRATES: 22g | SUGAR: 7g

Potato-Corn Chowder

This chowder is easily made vegetarian by swapping vegetable broth for chicken broth and omitting the bacon and chicken. I like using frozen corn while cooking for one because I can easily take out the portion I need without opening cans and having leftovers to worry about. If you can't find a small russet potato, you can also make this soup using frozen hash browns.

- **Hands-On Time: 5 minutes**
- **Cook Time: 11 minutes**

Serves 1

1 slice uncooked thick-cut bacon, diced

½ cup finely diced peeled potatoes

½ cup diced chicken breast in bite-sized pieces

¼ cup finely diced red bell pepper

1 teaspoon dried onion flakes

1½ cups chicken broth

½ cup frozen corn

¼ teaspoon salt

¼ teaspoon minced garlic

½ cup heavy cream

1 tablespoon all-purpose flour

1 On the Instant Pot®, press Sauté button and adjust to High. Add bacon and sauté about 5 minutes until crisp. Add potatoes, chicken, bell pepper, and onion flakes; sauté 1 minute. Press Cancel button to turn off the heat.

2 Add broth and deglaze the pot, scraping all the browned bits off the bottom of the pot. Add corn, salt, and garlic; stir.

3 Close the lid; turn the knob to Sealing.

4 Press Manual or Pressure Cook button and adjust time to 2 minutes.

5 When the timer beeps, immediately turn the knob from Sealing to Venting, then remove the lid. Press Sauté button and adjust to High.

6 In a small bowl, whisk cream and flour into a paste. Add it to soup and whisk about 3 minutes until thick. Transfer to a bowl and serve.

PER SERVING

CALORIES: 984 | FAT: 68g | PROTEIN: 42g | SODIUM: 2,442mg
FIBER: 3g | CARBOHYDRATES: 42g | SUGAR: 10g

Side Dishes for One

Side dishes are honestly one of the best parts of a meal, as they complement and enhance the main dish no matter how simple or fancy they are. The side dishes in this book are not incredibly fancy or time-consuming. Most of these recipes will teach you how to cook staple vegetable side dishes in the Instant Pot®, since they are the basic building blocks that every Instant Pot® owner should know how to make.

Making steamed broccoli has never been easier with my quick and foolproof method. Corn on the cob, potatoes, and green beans will never touch another pot or pan on the stovetop again. What you'll find when cooking vegetable side dishes in the Instant Pot® is that they take no time at all. Be careful not to overcook your vegetables and read the troubleshooting tips in the recipes.

My hope is that you'll find all of these side dishes to be great accompaniments to any recipe in this book, or a generous snack or full meal on their own. Armed with the skills and knowledge you'll gain in this chapter, you'll be ready to take on any recipe in your Instant Pot®, and even create your own.

Loaded Baked Potato Salad

Potato salad is a classic summer potluck dish, but if you're craving just a small portion, you can easily make this jazzed-up version with all your favorite loaded baked potato flavors—without the potluck!

- **Hands-On Time: 5 minutes**
- **Cook Time: 11 minutes**

Serves 1

1½ cups peeled and
    diced russet potatoes,
    cut into ½"–1" cubes
1 cup water
2 tablespoons mayonnaise
1½ tablespoons sour cream
¼ teaspoon seasoned salt
1⁄16 teaspoon ground
    black pepper
1⁄16 teaspoon smoked paprika
1 teaspoon dried chives
1 tablespoon bacon bits
1 tablespoon shredded
    Cheddar cheese

1 Place potatoes in a steamer basket. Pour water into Instant Pot®.

2 Place steamer basket into Instant Pot®.

3 Close the lid; turn the knob to Sealing.

4 Press Manual or Pressure Cook button and adjust time to 6 minutes.

5 When the timer beeps, allow 5 minutes to naturally release the pressure, then remove the lid.

6 Remove steamer basket and let potatoes cool in refrigerator while preparing the sauce.

7 In a medium bowl, mix together remaining ingredients, then add cool potatoes and mix. Chill in the refrigerator at least 1 hour or until ready to serve.

PER SERVING

CALORIES: 449 | **FAT:** 28g | **PROTEIN:** 9g | **SODIUM:** 777mg
FIBER: 3g | **CARBOHYDRATES:** 40g | **SUGAR:** 4g

Brown Sugar–Glazed Carrots

Whether you have a small bag of baby carrots in the refrigerator or you have some carrots left over from a vegetable tray, this is a fast and easy way to create a deliciously sweet and nostalgic side dish for one.

- Hands-On Time: 2 minutes
- Cook Time: 4 minutes

Serves 1

1 cup baby carrots
½ cup water
½ tablespoon butter
1 tablespoon brown sugar
½ tablespoon maple syrup
⅛ teaspoon salt

1 To the Instant Pot®, add carrots and water.

2 Close the lid; turn the knob to Sealing.

3 Press Manual or Pressure Cook button and adjust time to 1 minute.

4 When the timer beeps, immediately turn the knob from Sealing to Venting, then remove the lid and check carrots for doneness. If the carrots are not tender enough, replace lid, turn the knob to Sealing, and wait 2 minutes, then check again.

5 Drain water from Instant Pot®. Press Sauté button and adjust to High.

6 Add butter, brown sugar, maple syrup, and salt to carrots, and stir about 3 minutes until everything is melted and combined. Transfer to a plate and serve immediately.

PER SERVING

CALORIES: 180 | FAT: 6g | PROTEIN: 1g | SODIUM: 382mg
FIBER: 4g | CARBOHYDRATES: 33g | SUGAR: 26g

Buttery Smooth Mashed Potatoes

(pictured)

This recipe uses russet potatoes to produce a smooth, buttery, generous serving of mashed potatoes. If you'd like, garnish these with a sprinkle of chopped parsley.

- **Hands-On Time: 5 minutes**
- **Cook Time: 8 minutes**

Serves 1

1½ cups peeled and diced russet potatoes

1 cup chicken broth

1 tablespoon butter

3 tablespoons heavy cream

⅛ teaspoon salt

1⁄16 teaspoon ground black pepper

1 To the Instant Pot®, add potatoes and broth.

2 Close the lid; turn the knob to Sealing.

3 Press Manual or Pressure Cook button and adjust time to 8 minutes.

4 When the timer beeps, immediately turn the knob from Sealing to Venting, then remove the lid.

5 Drain potatoes into a medium bowl, then mash them with butter, cream, salt, and pepper. Transfer to a plate and serve.

PER SERVING

CALORIES: 440 | FAT: 27g | PROTEIN: 6g | SODIUM: 1,240mg
FIBER: 3g | CARBOHYDRATES: 42g | SUGAR: 5g

Simple Corn on the Cob

The Instant Pot® makes corn in mere minutes with almost no thought required so you can enjoy it anytime. If fresh corn is not available to you, this recipe can be used with frozen corn on the cob.

- **Hands-On Time: 2 minutes**
- **Cook Time: 3 minutes**

Serves 1

1 cup water

1 medium ear corn, husked

1 teaspoon butter

⅛ teaspoon salt

⅛ teaspoon ground black pepper

1 Pour water into Instant Pot® and add the trivet. Place corn on trivet.

2 Close the lid; turn the knob to Sealing.

3 Press Manual or Pressure Cook button and adjust time to 3 minutes.

4 When the timer beeps, immediately turn the knob from Sealing to Venting, then remove the lid and carefully transfer corn to a serving plate.

5 Spread butter over hot corn, then sprinkle with salt and pepper. Serve immediately.

PER SERVING

CALORIES: 131 | FAT: 5g | PROTEIN: 4g | SODIUM: 291mg
FIBER: 3g | CARBOHYDRATES: 22g | SUGAR: 5g

Crispy Baby Potatoes

You can purchase extra-small bags of baby potatoes, making this a perfect side dish for one. I prefer a mixed variety of potatoes, but you can use golden potatoes, red potatoes, or even fingerling potatoes. Just ensure the potatoes are halved at the widest point for maximum crispiness.

- **Hands-On Time: 5 minutes**
- **Cook Time: 13 minutes**

Serves 1

1 cup water
¼ teaspoon minced garlic
½ teaspoon salt
1½ cups halved baby potatoes
⅛ teaspoon kosher salt
⅛ teaspoon ground black pepper
½ teaspoon Old Bay seasoning
1 tablespoon butter

1 In the Instant Pot®, combine water, garlic, salt, and potatoes.

2 Close the lid; turn the knob to Sealing.

3 Press Manual or Pressure Cook button and adjust time to 5 minutes.

4 When the timer beeps, immediately turn the knob from Sealing to Venting, then remove the lid.

5 Drain potatoes into a small bowl and toss with salt, pepper, and Old Bay seasoning. Press Sauté button on the Instant Pot® and adjust to High.

6 When the Instant Pot® display reads "HOT," add butter and potatoes. Lay potatoes in the pot cut-side down. Do not flip or move potatoes until extremely crispy, about 5–8 minutes. Transfer to a serving plate and serve immediately.

PER SERVING

CALORIES: 275 | FAT: 11g | PROTEIN: 5g | SODIUM: 1,746mg
FIBER: 5g | CARBOHYDRATES: 40g | SUGAR: 2g

Upstate New York Salt Potatoes

A favorite of local upstate New Yorkers, salt potatoes are a summertime favorite. Baby potatoes cook in super-salty water, which makes the potatoes incredibly smooth and buttery on the inside, while creating a skin that "pops" on the outside. Most of the salt is not absorbed into the potatoes but rather forms a nice crust on the outside. This is a great accompaniment to any main protein or as a side to cheese fondue.

- Hands-On Time: 5 minutes
- Cook Time: 6 minutes

Serves 1

8 bite-sized potatoes
4 cups water
¾ cup salt
½ tablespoon butter, melted
⅛ teaspoon kosher salt
¼ teaspoon minced
 fresh parsley

1 To the Instant Pot®, add potatoes, water, and salt.

2 Close the lid; turn the knob to Sealing.

3 Press Manual or Pressure Cook button and adjust time to 6 minutes.

4 When the timer beeps, immediately turn the knob from Sealing to Venting, then remove the lid. Using a slotted spoon, carefully remove potatoes from water or drain in a colander.

5 Transfer to a serving plate. Drizzle potatoes with butter and sprinkle with salt and parsley. Serve immediately.

PER SERVING

CALORIES: 213 | FAT: 5g | PROTEIN: 4g | SODIUM: 4,542mg
FIBER: 3g | CARBOHYDRATES: 38g | SUGAR: 3g

Korean Sautéed Spinach

Since spinach cooks so quickly, this dish uses the Sauté feature of the Instant Pot® to bring you a deliciously savory, yet sweet Korean delicacy.

- **Hands-On Time: 1 minute**
- **Cook Time: 3 minutes**

Serves 1

1 tablespoon sesame oil
¼ teaspoon minced garlic
1 teaspoon dried onion flakes
2 cups packed spinach
1 teaspoon soy sauce
1 teaspoon sugar
¼ teaspoon sesame seeds

1 Press Sauté button on the Instant Pot® and adjust to High. Wait 1 minute for it to heat up. Add oil, garlic, and onion flakes, and stir 30 seconds.

2 Add spinach and cook 2 minutes until it wilts. Add soy sauce and sugar and stir another 30 seconds.

3 Remove to a serving bowl and top with sesame seeds. Serve.

PER SERVING

CALORIES: 160 | **FAT:** 14g | **PROTEIN:** 2g | **SODIUM:** 338mg
FIBER: 2g | **CARBOHYDRATES:** 8g | **SUGAR:** 5g

Creamy Cauliflower Puree

This is a low-carb favorite that is great served with a main dish protein or as a replacement for rice or mashed potatoes.

- **Hands-On Time: 5 minutes**
- **Cook Time: 5 minutes**

Serves 1

1½ cups cauliflower florets
½ cup chicken broth
⅛ teaspoon seasoned salt
2 tablespoons heavy cream
⅛ teaspoon garlic salt
1 tablespoon butter

1 To the Instant Pot®, add cauliflower and broth. Sprinkle seasoned salt over the cauliflower.

2 Close the lid; turn the knob to Sealing.

3 Press Manual or Pressure Cook button and adjust time to 5 minutes.

4 When the timer beeps, immediately turn the knob from Sealing to Venting, then remove the lid and drain broth from Instant Pot®.

5 Add cream, garlic salt, and butter to cauliflower and blend with an immersion blender until smooth. Transfer to a serving bowl and serve.

PER SERVING

CALORIES: 251 | **FAT:** 22g | **PROTEIN:** 5g | **SODIUM:** 956mg
FIBER: 3g | **CARBOHYDRATES:** 9g | **SUGAR:** 4g

Classic Potato Salad

The potatoes and egg cook at the same time in the Instant Pot® to make a quick and easy potato salad for one.

- **Hands-On Time: 5 minutes**
- **Cook Time: 11 minutes**

Serves 1

1½ cups peeled and
    diced russet potatoes,
    cut into ½"–1" cubes
1 large egg
1 cup water
¼ cup mayonnaise
1 tablespoon minced celery
½ teaspoon Dijon mustard
¼ teaspoon seasoned salt
½ teaspoon Old Bay seasoning
¹⁄₁₆ teaspoon smoked paprika

1 Place potatoes and egg in a steamer basket. Pour water into Instant Pot®.

2 Place steamer basket into Instant Pot®.

3 Close the lid; turn the knob to Sealing.

4 Press Manual or Pressure Cook button and adjust time to 6 minutes.

5 When the timer beeps, allow 5 minutes to naturally release the pressure, then remove the lid.

6 Remove steamer basket and let potatoes cool in the refrigerator while assembling other ingredients. Remove egg to an ice bath and cool 5 minutes. Peel and chop once cool.

7 In a small bowl, mix together remaining ingredients, then add cool potatoes and chopped egg and combine. Chill in refrigerator at least 1 hour or until ready to serve.

PER SERVING

CALORIES: 622 | FAT: 45g | PROTEIN: 11g | SODIUM: 1,158mg
FIBER: 3g | CARBOHYDRATES: 41g | SUGAR: 4g

Broccoli with Brown Butter and Mizithra Cheese

Broccoli is a great side dish to cook for one because you can almost always purchase broccoli stalks or individual broccoli crowns from the bulk produce section at the grocery store, or you can purchase small bags of precut and washed broccoli for less waste. Make sure you brown the butter until it is dark golden brown and very nutty smelling; otherwise, the butter won't give enough flavor to the dish.

- **Hands-On Time: 3 minutes**
- **Cook Time: 0 minutes**

Serves 1

2 cups broccoli florets
1 cup water
2 tablespoons grated mizithra cheese
⅛ teaspoon salt
1½ tablespoons brown butter

0 MINUTE COOK TIME

The 0 minute cook time on the Instant Pot® allows the pot to come to pressure, then immediately turns off and begins naturally releasing the pressure. Since the pressure release always takes at least 30 seconds, the food in the Instant Pot® continues to cook using residual heat during this time. It's perfect for extremely delicate and quick cooking foods such as vegetables and seafood.

1 Place broccoli in a steamer basket or net (anything to keep the broccoli out of the water). Pour water into Instant Pot®.

2 Place steamer basket into Instant Pot®.

3 Close the lid; turn the knob to Sealing.

4 Press Manual or Pressure Cook button and adjust time to 0 minutes.

5 When the timer beeps, immediately turn the knob from Sealing to Venting, then remove the lid. Using a slotted spoon, carefully transfer the broccoli to a serving plate.

6 Sprinkle mizithra and salt over broccoli, then drizzle with brown butter. Serve immediately.

PER SERVING

CALORIES: 275 | FAT: 24g | PROTEIN: 8g | SODIUM: 710mg
FIBER: 5g | CARBOHYDRATES: 12g | SUGAR: 3g

Smoky Bacon Brussels Sprouts

Brussels sprouts are the perfect side dish for one because not only are they healthy and delicious; they're also almost always available in bulk or in small bags, allowing you to purchase only what you need for minimal waste.

- **Hands-On Time: 5 minutes**
- **Cook Time: 9 minutes**

Serves 1

1 slice uncooked thick-cut bacon, diced
1 tablespoon butter
2 cups Brussels sprouts, cut in half through the stem
⅛ teaspoon seasoned salt
⅛ teaspoon ground black pepper
⅛ teaspoon smoked paprika
½ cup chicken broth
¼ teaspoon minced garlic
½ teaspoon soy sauce
1 teaspoon dried onion flakes

CRISPY BRUSSELS SPROUTS

These yummy Brussels sprouts are fantastic as is, but to take them to another level, try crisping them up after pressure cooking. Here's how: Remove the contents of the Instant Pot®. Press Sauté button and adjust to High. Add an additional 1–2 tablespoons olive oil or butter to the pot. Using a slotted spoon, add Brussels sprouts and spread them evenly in the pot, cut-side down. Let them sauté 5–8 minutes until crispy. They're fantastic!

1 On the Instant Pot®, press Sauté button and adjust to High.

2 Add bacon and sauté about 5 minutes until crisp. Using a slotted spoon, remove bacon and set aside, leaving the bacon grease in the pot. Add butter and let melt.

3 Add Brussels sprouts and sprinkle with salt, pepper, and paprika. Sauté 3 minutes. Add broth and deglaze the pot, scraping all the browned bits off the bottom of the pot. Press Cancel button to turn off the heat, and sprinkle Brussels sprouts with garlic, soy sauce, onion flakes, and reserved bacon. Stir to combine.

4 Close the lid; turn the knob to Sealing.

5 Press Manual or Pressure Cook button and adjust time to 1 minute.

6 When the timer beeps, immediately turn the knob from Sealing to Venting, then remove the lid and carefully transfer sprouts to a serving plate. Serve.

PER SERVING

CALORIES: 422 | **FAT:** 32g | **PROTEIN:** 14g | **SODIUM:** 1,211mg
FIBER: 7g | **CARBOHYDRATES:** 19g | **SUGAR:** 5g

Cheesy Twice-Baked Potato

Making twice-baked potatoes in the oven is an all-night affair. The Instant Pot® takes a single potato and transforms it into one of the most popular side dishes in half the time.

- **Hands-On Time: 10 minutes**
- **Cook Time: 40 minutes**

Serves 1

1 cup water
1 large (about ½-pound) unpeeled russet potato
1 tablespoon whole milk
½ tablespoon butter
2 tablespoons sour cream
1 tablespoon softened cream cheese
3 tablespoons shredded Cheddar cheese, divided
⅛ teaspoon salt
⅛ teaspoon ground black pepper
¼ teaspoon dried chives
1 tablespoon bacon bits
½ teaspoon minced green onion

USING A KNIFE VERSUS SPOON

In my testing, the potatoes looked the best when they were cut out of the skin with a knife and gently scooped if necessary with a spoon.

1 Pour water into Instant Pot® and add the trivet. Place potato on trivet.

2 Close the lid; turn the knob to Sealing.

3 Press Manual or Pressure Cook button and adjust time to 25 minutes.

4 When the timer beeps, allow 5 minutes to naturally release the pressure, then remove the lid.

5 Preheat oven to 400°F. Line a baking sheet with foil.

6 Carefully remove potato from Instant Pot® and cut in half. Cool 5 minutes. Using a knife, cut out the potato flesh, leaving ¼"–½" of flesh in the potato skin. Carefully scoop out any remnants with a spoon into a small bowl.

7 To the small bowl, add milk, butter, sour cream, cream cheese, 2 tablespoons Cheddar, salt, pepper, and chives. Mash together until smooth.

8 Scoop potato mixture into the two potato skin halves, mounding the filling and gently patting it down.

9 Top each half with remaining ½ tablespoon Cheddar and bacon bits. Place on prepared baking sheet and bake 10 minutes until cheese is melted and bubbly.

10 Transfer potato halves to a serving plate. Top with green onion and serve immediately.

PER SERVING

CALORIES: 560 | FAT: 23g | PROTEIN: 18g | SODIUM: 696mg
FIBER: 7g | CARBOHYDRATES: 67g | SUGAR: 5g

Classic Steamed Artichoke

Dipped in butter or mayonnaise, a single artichoke is the best, easiest side dish! Just remember that if you don't cook an artichoke long enough, there won't be any "meat" to scrape off the leaves. The longer they cook, the more enjoyable they are. I have a full post on how to cook and eat an artichoke on my website, https://triedtestedandtrue.com/instant-pot-artichokes.

- **Hands-On Time: 1 minute**
- **Cook Time: 28 minutes**

Serves 1

1 cup water
1 medium (about ¾ pound) artichoke
3 tablespoons butter, melted

HOW TO EAT AN ARTICHOKE

Start by peeling off the outer leaves of the artichoke. These are the toughest, and there won't be much flesh on these. Dip the base of the leaf in butter or mayonnaise, then draw the leaf through your teeth, scraping off any available flesh. Discard whatever you can't eat. Keep going all the way around the artichoke until you're at the heart. Then you'll find a fuzzy layer called the choke. This part is not edible, so scrape this all out with a spoon. Under the choke is the heart—the best part of the artichoke! Simply cut the solid base into pieces and enjoy dipped in butter.

1 Pour water into Instant Pot® and add the trivet.

2 Cut bottom stem off artichoke, then slice off top ¼ of artichoke and discard. Using sharp scissors, trim the tips of the outer leaves.

3 Place artichoke upright on trivet.

4 Close the lid; turn the knob to Sealing.

5 Press Manual or Pressure Cook button and adjust time to 28 minutes.

6 When the timer beeps, immediately turn the knob from Sealing to Venting, then remove the lid and carefully transfer artichoke to a serving plate. Serve with butter.

PER SERVING

CALORIES: 368 | FAT: 32g | PROTEIN: 4g | SODIUM: 76mg
FIBER: 10g | CARBOHYDRATES: 14g | SUGAR: 1g

Sweet Potato Mash

Sweet potatoes are a healthy vegetable packed with tons of vitamins and nutrients. I love subbing them for carrots or potatoes whenever I can. This Sweet Potato Mash is creamy, smooth, and reminiscent of the traditional sweet potato casserole without as many calories.

- **Hands-On Time: 5 minutes**
- **Cook Time: 10 minutes**

Serves 1

1¼ cups diced sweet potatoes
1 cup water
1½ tablespoons brown sugar
¼ cup whole milk
⅛ teaspoon ground cinnamon

1 Place sweet potato cubes in a steamer basket.

2 Pour water into Instant Pot® and add the basket.

3 Close the lid; turn the knob to Sealing.

4 Press Manual or Pressure Cook button and adjust time to 10 minutes.

5 When the timer beeps, immediately turn the knob from Sealing to Venting, then remove the lid. Drain and rinse the Instant Pot® liner and pour sweet potato cubes from the steamer basket into the pot.

6 Add brown sugar, milk, and cinnamon. Using a potato masher or handheld electric mixer, mash until smooth and fluffy. Transfer to a serving bowl and serve.

PER SERVING

CALORIES: 257 | FAT: 2g | PROTEIN: 5g | SODIUM: 122mg
FIBER: 5g | CARBOHYDRATES: 57g | SUGAR: 30g

Sweet Potato Casserole with Brown Sugar Pecan Crust

This dish is a holiday favorite that you can now make as a mini casserole just for yourself! Try using precut sweet potato cubes to save time and prevent waste, or use small sweet potatoes that you pressure-cook whole (about 2 small potatoes).

- **Hands-On Time: 10 minutes**
- **Cook Time: 40 minutes**

Serves 1

Casserole
1¼ cups diced sweet potatoes
1 cup water
1½ tablespoons brown sugar
¼ cup heavy cream
⅛ teaspoon ground cinnamon
½ teaspoon vanilla extract
¼ teaspoon salt
1 large egg

Topping
1½ tablespoons brown sugar
1½ tablespoons granulated sugar
1½ tablespoons all-purpose flour
1½ tablespoons chopped pecans
1 tablespoon butter
1/16 teaspoon ground cinnamon

BAKE IN THE AIR FRYER
When making small dishes, I like to use the air fryer so I don't have to turn on my oven for just one thing. Preheat the air fryer to 325°F and bake this casserole 30 minutes until browned and bubbly. Transfer to a serving bowl and serve.

1 Preheat oven to 350°F. Grease a 6" cake pan or ovenproof casserole dish. Set aside.

2 Place sweet potato cubes in a steamer basket.

3 Pour water into Instant Pot® and add the basket. Close the lid; turn the knob to Sealing.

4 Press Manual or Pressure Cook button and adjust time to 10 minutes.

5 When the timer beeps, immediately turn the knob from Sealing to Venting, then remove the lid. Drain and rinse the Instant Pot® liner and pour sweet potato cubes from the steamer basket into the pot.

6 Add brown sugar, cream, cinnamon, vanilla, salt, and egg. Using a potato masher or handheld electric mixer, mash until smooth and fluffy.

7 Pour mixture into prepared cake pan or casserole dish.

8 In a medium bowl, using a pastry blender or fork, mix together all Topping ingredients until mixture resembles large crumbs. Crumble evenly over the casserole.

9 Bake 20–30 minutes until crust is browned and casserole is bubbly on the edges. Serve.

PER SERVING
CALORIES: 865 | **FAT:** 43g | **PROTEIN:** 12g | **SODIUM:** 776mg **FIBER:** 7g | **CARBOHYDRATES:** 106g | **SUGAR:** 68g

Steamed Spaghetti Squash

Spaghetti squash can take well over 90 minutes to roast in the oven. No way! Now I put a whole small spaghetti squash in the Instant Pot®, and in half an hour, I have enough squash for two meals. One small spaghetti squash yields about 4 cups total. Make sure to also try the Spaghetti Squash with Lemon-Cream Sauce in Chapter 9 or Creamy Spicy Italian Sausage and Spaghetti Squash "Pasta" in Chapter 6.

- **Hands-On Time: 2 minutes**
- **Cook Time: 25 minutes**

Serves 1

1 cup water
1 small spaghetti squash

HOW TO SERVE SPAGHETTI SQUASH

This vegetable is light and healthy! When cooked properly, it'll separate into a bunch of yellow strands that look like (but don't taste like) spaghetti noodles! I often use this as a low-carb replacement for pasta or in casseroles or stir-fries as a filler. It's also excellent on its own with a drizzle of olive oil or butter and some Parmesan cheese and salt.

1 Pour water into Instant Pot® and add the trivet. Place spaghetti squash on trivet.

2 Close the lid; turn the knob to Sealing.

3 Press Manual or Pressure Cook button and adjust time to 25 minutes.

4 When the timer beeps, immediately turn the knob from Sealing to Venting, then remove the lid and carefully transfer squash to a cutting board. Cool 10 minutes.

5 Carefully slice squash in half. Cutting squash through the stem will result in shorter strands, while cutting crosswise through the middle will result in longer strands. Scoop out seeds from each half and discard. Using tongs or a fork, gently scrape and pull squash strands out of the shell and into a serving dish. Serve.

PER SERVING

CALORIES: 125 | FAT: 2g | PROTEIN: 3g | SODIUM: 68mg
FIBER: 6g | CARBOHYDRATES: 28g | SUGAR: 11g

Personal Green Bean Casserole

This crispy, creamy green bean holiday casserole can now be enjoyed year-round in your own personal pan! Rather than waste most of a can of a cream-of-something soup, you can make this casserole with a scratch-made sauce, reducing waste and controlling all the flavor and sodium.

- **Hands-On Time: 15 minutes**
- **Cook Time: 30 minutes**

Serves 1

1 teaspoon butter
1 teaspoon all-purpose flour
1 teaspoon dried onion flakes
¼ teaspoon minced garlic
¼ teaspoon soy sauce
¼ cup whole milk
¼ cup chicken broth
2 tablespoons sour cream
1 (14-ounce) can green beans, drained
1 cup water
½ cup packaged French fried onions

1 Grease a 6" cake pan. Set aside.

2 In a small saucepan over medium heat, melt butter and add flour. Whisk together about 2 minutes to make a light roux. Add onion flakes, garlic, and soy sauce. Slowly whisk in milk and broth and cook about 3 minutes until thickened. Remove from heat and add sour cream and green beans.

3 Transfer mixture to prepared cake pan and cover with foil.

4 Pour water into Instant Pot® and add the trivet. Place pan on trivet.

5 Close the lid; turn the knob to Sealing.

6 Press Manual or Pressure Cook button and adjust time to 20 minutes.

7 When the timer beeps, immediately turn the knob from Sealing to Venting, then remove the lid. Carefully remove pan from Instant Pot® and remove foil.

8 Preheat oven or air fryer to 350°F.

9 Sprinkle French fried onions on top of casserole and bake 5 minutes until crispy. Transfer to a serving bowl and serve.

PER SERVING

CALORIES: 364 | FAT: 24g | PROTEIN: 6g | SODIUM: 1,122mg
FIBER: 5g | CARBOHYDRATES: 29g | SUGAR: 6g

Savory Bacon Green Beans

Bacon, green beans, and mushrooms come together in a light savory sauce for a delicious dish. One of my friends said these were the best green beans she'd ever had!

- **Hands-On Time: 5 minutes**
- **Cook Time: 12 minutes**

Serves 1

1 slice uncooked thick-cut bacon, chopped

⅓ cup diced mushrooms

½ tablespoon dried onion flakes

½ teaspoon minced garlic

¼ cup chicken broth

½ teaspoon soy sauce

5 ounces fresh green beans, trimmed

1 On the Instant Pot®, press Sauté button and adjust to High.

2 Add bacon and sauté about 5 minutes until crispy. Add mushrooms, onion flakes, garlic, broth, and soy sauce. Press Cancel button to turn off the heat, and deglaze the pot, scraping all the browned bits off the bottom of the pot. Add green beans and stir.

3 Close the lid; turn the knob to Sealing.

4 Press Manual or Pressure Cook button and adjust time to 2 minutes.

5 When the timer beeps, allow 5 minutes to naturally release the pressure, then remove the lid. Transfer to a serving bowl and serve immediately.

PER SERVING

CALORIES: 295 | **FAT:** 21g | **PROTEIN:** 11g | **SODIUM:** 754mg
FIBER: 4g | **CARBOHYDRATES:** 14g | **SUGAR:** 7g

5

Snacks and Appetizers

The snacks and appetizers in this chapter are so, so good! Can we agree that some things are just better miniature-sized? (Thanks, Personal Pan Pizza!) These scaled-down versions of the classics are perfect because you won't be tempted to eat an entire casserole dish's worth of a creamy corn dip, and you can prepare multiple dishes to make yourself a little sampler plate. After all, isn't the sampler the most popular appetizer at any restaurant?

If you ever get a hankering for deviled eggs, try the new and inventive variations in this chapter, like Bacon-Chive Deviled Eggs and Jalapeño-Ranch Deviled Eggs (which even includes potato chips!). The Spicy Sausage Dip and Creamy Chili-Cheese Dip make great use of leftover ingredients from other recipes, while the Jalapeño Popper Dip and Creamy Corn Dip will knock your socks off. If you're short on time, try the Easy Frozen Pot Stickers with Sesame-Soy Dipping Sauce!

If you're looking for a sweet snack, try making my easy Spiced Vanilla-Pear Sauce, which is delicious on its own hot or cold, or spooned over a cake or ice cream.

Easy Frozen Pot Stickers with Sesame-Soy Dipping Sauce

You can enjoy frozen pot stickers as an appetizer, snack, or full meal! If you want to have just a couple of these as a snack, the Instant Pot® makes it incredibly easy to steam frozen pot stickers in a flash without having to wait 15-plus minutes to make them on the stove. The chili oil is optional; feel free to eliminate it if you don't like it.

- **Hands-On Time: 5 minutes**
- **Cook Time: 3 minutes**

Serves 1

Pot Stickers
1 cup water
5 frozen pot stickers
1 teaspoon chopped green onion
½ tablespoon sesame seeds

Sesame-Soy Dipping Sauce
1 tablespoon soy sauce
1 tablespoon rice wine vinegar
1 teaspoon sesame oil
⅛ teaspoon grated fresh ginger
⅛ teaspoon minced garlic
¼ teaspoon chopped green onion
1/16 teaspoon crushed red pepper flakes
⅛ teaspoon chili oil

1 To the Instant Pot®, add water and pot stickers.

2 Close the lid; turn the knob to Sealing.

3 Press Manual or Pressure Cook button and adjust time to 3 minutes.

4 In a small bowl, mix together all Sesame-Soy Dipping Sauce ingredients while pot stickers cook.

5 When the timer beeps, immediately turn the knob from Sealing to Venting, then remove the lid. Using a slotted spoon, carefully transfer pot stickers to a serving plate. Garnish with green onion, sesame seeds, and serve with Sesame-Soy Dipping Sauce.

PER SERVING

CALORIES: 276 | FAT: 14g | PROTEIN: 14g | SODIUM: 1,517mg
FIBER: 3g | CARBOHYDRATES: 22g | SUGAR: 4g

Homemade Cinnamon Applesauce

Traditional applesauce recipes will make you enough applesauce to last months! If you only want a single portion, this is the perfect recipe. Try making this simple Instant Pot® applesauce if you have some leftover apples or want to add a delicious snack to your day.

- **Hands-On Time: 5 minutes**
- **Cook Time: 25 minutes**

Serves 1

1 medium Granny Smith apple, peeled, cored, and sliced

1 medium Honeycrisp apple, peeled, cored, and sliced

½ tablespoon lemon juice

¼ teaspoon ground cinnamon

½ cup water

1 tablespoon sugar

1 To the Instant Pot®, add apples, lemon juice, cinnamon, and water.

2 Close the lid; turn the knob to Sealing.

3 Press Manual or Pressure Cook button and adjust time to 10 minutes.

4 When the timer beeps, allow 15 minutes to naturally release the pressure, then remove the lid.

5 Stir applesauce until well combined, then carefully taste. Add up to 1 tablespoon sugar or more, depending on your taste. The amount of sugar you use will vary, depending on the sweetness and tartness of your apples. Transfer to a bowl and serve.

PER SERVING

CALORIES: 204 | FAT: 0g | PROTEIN: 1g | SODIUM: 0mg
FIBER: 5g | CARBOHYDRATES: 55g | SUGAR: 45g

Spiced Vanilla-Pear Sauce

This sauce can be eaten alone or scooped over vanilla ice cream or pound cake for a delicious treat.

- **Hands-On Time: 5 minutes**
- **Cook Time: 10 minutes**

Serves 1

3 medium ripe pears, peeled, cored, and diced
⅛ teaspoon ground cinnamon
1⁄16 teaspoon ground ginger
1⁄16 teaspoon ground cloves
1⁄16 teaspoon ground nutmeg
⅓ cup apple juice
½ teaspoon vanilla extract

1 In the Instant Pot®, combine pears, cinnamon, ginger, cloves, nutmeg, and apple juice.

2 Close the lid; turn the knob to Sealing.

3 Press Manual or Pressure Cook button and adjust time to 10 minutes.

4 When the timer beeps, immediately turn the knob from Sealing to Venting, then remove the lid.

5 Using a whisk or potato masher, stir the pear sauce together until all the pears are broken up and the consistency is like applesauce. Stir in vanilla and transfer to a bowl. Serve warm, or chill in the refrigerator until ready to serve.

PER SERVING

CALORIES: 324 | FAT: 1g | PROTEIN: 2g | SODIUM: 8mg
FIBER: 11g | CARBOHYDRATES: 85g | SUGAR: 60g

Sweet and Smoky Cocktail Sausages

This yummy sweet and savory appetizer is a super-easy one-and-done snack that everyone loves!

- **Hands-On Time: 3 minutes**
- **Cook Time: 15 minutes**

Serves 1

1 cup water
½ (14-ounce) package cocktail sausages
2 tablespoons barbecue sauce
¼ cup grape jelly

1 Pour water into Instant Pot® and add the trivet.

2 Add all remaining ingredients to a 6" cake pan and cover with foil. Place pan on trivet.

3 Close the lid; turn the knob to Sealing.

4 Press Manual or Pressure Cook button and adjust time to 15 minutes.

5 When the timer beeps, immediately turn the knob from Sealing to Venting, then remove the lid and carefully transfer sausages to a serving plate. Serve.

PER SERVING

CALORIES: 871 | FAT: 52g | PROTEIN: 25g | SODIUM: 2,358mg
FIBER: 1g | CARBOHYDRATES: 72g | SUGAR: 50g

Cocktail Shrimp

Treat yourself with a personal serving of cocktail shrimp, cooked überquick in the Instant Pot®.

- **Hands-On Time: 5 minutes**
- **Cook Time: 0 minutes**

Serves 1

1 cup water
½ teaspoon salt
2 cups frozen peeled and deveined jumbo shrimp
2 tablespoons cocktail sauce
½ medium lemon

1 To the Instant Pot®, add water, salt, and shrimp.

2 Close the lid; turn the knob to Sealing.

3 Press Manual or Pressure Cook button and adjust time to 0 minutes.

4 When the timer beeps, immediately turn the knob from Sealing to Venting, then remove the lid and drain shrimp. Place shrimp in an ice bath 5 minutes to halt the cooking process.

5 Remove to a serving bowl and serve with cocktail sauce and lemon.

PER SERVING

CALORIES: 218 | FAT: 2g | PROTEIN: 47g | SODIUM: 2,335mg
FIBER: 1g | CARBOHYDRATES: 13g | SUGAR: 4g

Easy-Peel Hard-Boiled Eggs

Hard-boiled eggs can be made in the Instant Pot® in any quantity—the cook time stays the same.

- **Hands-On Time: 1 minute**
- **Cook Time: 16 minutes**

Serves 1

1 cup water
2 large eggs
⅛ teaspoon salt

1 Pour water into Instant Pot® and add the trivet.

2 Place eggs on trivet.

3 Close the lid; turn the knob to Sealing.

4 Press Manual or Pressure Cook button and adjust time to 2 minutes.

5 When the timer beeps, allow 14 minutes to naturally release the pressure, then remove the lid.

6 Immediately place the eggs in an ice bath 10 minutes. Peel and transfer to a bowl. Serve with salt.

PER SERVING

CALORIES: 155 | FAT: 9g | PROTEIN: 13g | SODIUM: 414mg
FIBER: 0g | CARBOHYDRATES: 1g | SUGAR: 1g

Classic Deviled Eggs for One

This recipe is perfect for when you have a craving for a delicious classic deviled egg but don't have the occasion to make a full batch.

- **Hands-On Time: 5 minutes**
- **Cook Time: 16 minutes**

Serves 1

1 cup water
2 large eggs
1 tablespoon mayonnaise
⅛ teaspoon yellow mustard
1/16 teaspoon salt
1/16 teaspoon ground
   black pepper
1/16 teaspoon smoked paprika

OVERCOOKED EGGS?

If your eggs are super chalky and have a gray ring around the yolk, they are overcooked. Try shaving 1–3 minutes off the natural pressure release time and be sure to cool them down as soon as possible to stop the cooking process.

1 Pour water into Instant Pot® and add the trivet. Place eggs on trivet.

2 Close the lid; turn the knob to Sealing.

3 Press Manual or Pressure Cook button and adjust time to 2 minutes.

4 When the timer beeps, allow 14 minutes to naturally release the pressure, then remove the lid.

5 Immediately place eggs in an ice bath and cool 10 minutes. Peel, cut in half lengthwise, then remove yolks to a small bowl. Place halved egg whites on a small plate.

6 Using a fork or whisk, break up egg yolks until very fine and crumbly. Mix in mayonnaise, mustard, salt, and pepper until smooth.

7 Fill egg white halves with egg yolk mixture and top with paprika. Transfer to a serving plate and serve.

PER SERVING

CALORIES: 248 | FAT: 19g | PROTEIN: 13g | SODIUM: 362mg
FIBER: 0g | CARBOHYDRATES: 1g | SUGAR: 1g

Bacon-Chive Deviled Eggs

These smoky, oniony, and completely delicious Bacon-Chive Deviled Eggs will be your new go-to for a quick and easy yet elevated appetizer. Garnish them with a little fresh chive for an elegant flair.

- **Hands-On Time: 5 minutes**
- **Cook Time: 16 minutes**

Serves 1

1 cup water
2 large eggs
1 tablespoon mayonnaise
1 teaspoon bacon bits
1/8 teaspoon dried chives
1/16 teaspoon salt
1/16 teaspoon ground black pepper

1 Pour water into Instant Pot® and add the trivet. Place eggs on trivet.

2 Close the lid; turn the knob to Sealing.

3 Press Manual or Pressure Cook button and adjust time to 2 minutes.

4 When the timer beeps, allow 14 minutes to naturally release the pressure, then remove the lid.

5 Immediately place the eggs in an ice bath 10 minutes. Peel, cut in half lengthwise, then remove the yolks to a small bowl. Place halved egg whites on a small plate.

6 Using a fork or whisk, break up egg yolks until very fine and crumbly. Mix in mayonnaise, bacon bits, chives, salt, and pepper until smooth.

7 Fill egg white halves with egg yolk mixture. Transfer to a serving plate and serve.

PER SERVING

CALORIES: 258 | FAT: 20g | PROTEIN: 14g | SODIUM: 409mg
FIBER: 0g | CARBOHYDRATES: 1g | SUGAR: 1g

Jalapeño-Ranch Deviled Eggs

These deviled eggs are the perfect blend of heat, crunch, and creaminess—a great way to start off any meal or snack.

- **Hands-On Time: 5 minutes**
- **Cook Time: 16 minutes**

Serves 1

1 cup water
2 large eggs
1 tablespoon ranch dressing
1/16 teaspoon salt
1/16 teaspoon ground
    black pepper
4 slices pickled
    jalapeño pepper
4 small potato chips

1 Pour water into Instant Pot® and add the trivet. Place eggs on trivet.

2 Close the lid; turn the knob to Sealing.

3 Press Manual or Pressure Cook button and adjust time to 2 minutes.

4 When the timer beeps, allow 14 minutes to naturally release the pressure, then remove the lid.

5 Immediately place eggs in an ice bath and cool 10 minutes. Peel, cut in half lengthwise, then remove yolks to a small bowl. Place halved egg whites on a small plate.

6 Using a fork or whisk, break up egg yolks until very fine and crumbly. Mix in ranch, salt, and pepper until smooth.

7 Fill egg white halves with egg yolk mixture and top each egg with a jalapeño slice and potato chip. Transfer to a serving plate and serve.

PER SERVING

CALORIES: 278 | **FAT:** 19g | **PROTEIN:** 13g | **SODIUM:** 478mg
FIBER: 0g | **CARBOHYDRATES:** 7g | **SUGAR:** 1g

Jalapeño Popper Dip

Jalapeño poppers are usually halved jalapeño peppers stuffed with a mixture of cream cheese and Cheddar and wrapped in bacon. However delicious they are, they are a bit time-consuming to make, especially if you want only a small batch. This dip makes it possible to throw together all the same ingredients and flavors in an easy and quick appetizer or snack for one.

- **Hands-On Time: 10 minutes**
- **Cook Time: 20 minutes**

Serves 1

2 ounces cream cheese, softened

4 tablespoons shredded Cheddar cheese, divided

2 tablespoons minced pickled jalapeño peppers

1 tablespoon sour cream

4 teaspoons bacon bits

$\frac{1}{16}$ teaspoon salt

$\frac{1}{16}$ teaspoon garlic powder

3 slices pickled jalapeño peppers

1 cup water

1 Grease an 8-ounce ramekin. Set aside.

2 In a small bowl, combine cream cheese, 3 tablespoons Cheddar, minced jalapeños, sour cream, bacon bits, salt, and garlic powder. Spoon the mixture into prepared ramekin and place the jalapeño slices on top, cover with foil.

3 Pour water into Instant Pot® and add the trivet. Place ramekin on trivet.

4 Close the lid; turn the knob to Sealing.

5 Press Manual or Pressure Cook button and adjust time to 15 minutes.

6 When the timer beeps, immediately turn the knob from Sealing to Venting, then remove the lid and carefully remove ramekin to an ovenproof plate.

7 Preheat oven broiler or air fryer to high.

8 Remove foil from dip and sprinkle the top with remaining 1 tablespoon Cheddar.

9 Broil 3–5 minutes until browned on top. Serve immediately.

PER SERVING

CALORIES: 370 | FAT: 30g | PROTEIN: 14g | SODIUM: 1,012mg
FIBER: 0g | CARBOHYDRATES: 3g | SUGAR: 2g

Creamy Buffalo Chicken Dip

Whether it's to enjoy while watching a big game or as a simple delicious appetizer or snack, this Creamy Buffalo Chicken Dip is just the right thing to satisfy any buffalo craving! I recommend using Frank's RedHot Buffalo Wings Sauce in this recipe. Serve with potato chips, chopped vegetables, in a lettuce wrap, or with pretzels.

- **Hands-On Time: 8 minutes**
- **Cook Time: 30 minutes**

Serves 1

1 (8-ounce) boneless, skinless chicken breast

1 cup water

$\frac{1}{16}$ teaspoon salt

$\frac{1}{16}$ teaspoon ground black pepper

2 ounces cream cheese, softened

2 tablespoons buffalo sauce

1 teaspoon dry ranch seasoning

$1\frac{1}{2}$ tablespoons shredded Cheddar cheese

1 tablespoon chopped green onion

1 To the Instant Pot®, add chicken and water. Season chicken with salt and pepper.

2 Close the lid; turn the knob to Sealing.

3 Press Manual or Pressure Cook button and adjust time to 20 minutes.

4 When the timer beeps, allow 10 minutes to naturally release the pressure, then remove the lid.

5 Remove chicken to a small bowl and add 1 tablespoon cooking liquid. Using two forks, shred the chicken.

6 Add remaining ingredients and mix thoroughly. Transfer to a serving bowl and serve immediately.

PER SERVING

CALORIES: 275 | **FAT:** 20g | **PROTEIN:** 12g | **SODIUM:** 1,651mg **FIBER:** 0g | **CARBOHYDRATES:** 5g | **SUGAR:** 2g

Spicy Sausage Dip

A hearty, spicy, and creamy dip that's the perfect accompaniment to a crusty loaf of bread. I like to make this dip when I purchase a pound of Italian sausage to make Zuppa Toscana or Cheesy Lasagna Soup (see recipes in Chapter 3).

- **Hands-On Time: 10 minutes**
- **Cook Time: 25 minutes**

Serves 1

2 ounces cream cheese, softened

3 tablespoons Rotel Diced Tomatoes and Green Chilies

½ cup cooked and crumbled Italian sausage

3 tablespoons shredded Cheddar cheese, divided

1 cup water

1 Grease an 8-ounce ramekin. Set aside.

2 In a small bowl, combine cream cheese, tomatoes and chilies, sausage, and 2 table-spoons Cheddar. Spoon into prepared ramekin and cover with foil.

3 Pour water into Instant Pot® and add the trivet. Place ramekin on trivet.

4 Close the lid; turn the knob to Sealing.

5 Press Manual or Pressure Cook button and adjust time to 20 minutes.

6 When the timer beeps, immediately turn the knob from Sealing to Venting, then remove the lid and carefully remove ramekin to an ovenproof plate.

7 Uncover dip and sprinkle the top with remaining 1 tablespoon Cheddar.

8 Preheat oven broiler or air fryer to high.

9 Broil 3–5 minutes until browned on top. Serve immediately.

PER SERVING

CALORIES: 483 | FAT: 38g | PROTEIN: 19g | SODIUM: 1,168mg
FIBER: 0g | CARBOHYDRATES: 7g | SUGAR: 3g

Herb and Cheese–Stuffed Artichoke

This fancy-yet-simple appetizer is a favorite Italian classic. A whole artichoke is stuffed with bread crumbs, cheese, and herbs, and topped with lemon juice and butter for a delicious and fun appetizer for one. This recipe uses panko bread crumbs for a lighter texture.

- **Hands-On Time: 5 minutes**
- **Cook Time: 45 minutes**

Serves 1

1 cup water
1 large (over 1-pound) artichoke
2 tablespoons panko bread crumbs
½ teaspoon Italian seasoning
½ teaspoon minced garlic
2 tablespoons grated Parmesan cheese
1 tablespoon lemon juice
3 tablespoons butter, melted, divided

TRIMMING ARTICHOKES

The leaves on an artichoke can be extremely sharp! I suggest trimming all the leaves on the outside of the artichoke with sharp scissors or a serrated knife and taking great care while cutting the artichoke and when handling the discarded leaves.

1 Pour water into Instant Pot® and add the trivet.

2 Cut the bottom stem off artichoke, then slice off the top ¼ of artichoke and discard. Using sharp scissors, trim the tips of the outer leaves.

3 Gently spread the leaves to fan the artichoke out and create gaps between the leaves.

4 In a small bowl, toss together bread crumbs, Italian seasoning, garlic, and Parmesan. Using your fingers or a spoon, sprinkle bread crumb mixture over the top of artichoke and gently press down between the leaves. Place artichoke on trivet.

5 Close the lid; turn the knob to Sealing.

6 Press Manual or Pressure Cook button and adjust time to 45 minutes.

7 When the timer beeps, immediately turn the knob from Sealing to Venting, then remove the lid and carefully transfer artichoke to a serving plate.

8 Drizzle with lemon juice and 1 tablespoon butter. Serve with remaining 2 tablespoons butter for dipping.

PER SERVING

CALORIES: 478 | **FAT:** 35g | **PROTEIN:** 10g | **SODIUM:** 363mg
FIBER: 9g | **CARBOHYDRATES:** 30g | **SUGAR:** 3g

Spinach-Artichoke Dip

Not only is it easier to make a single serving of this delicious appetizer, but it's also a lot easier to control the portion size of this indulgent, creamy treat. I like to bake mine in the air fryer after it's done cooking for a crispier crust, but if you like a smoother dip, feel free to omit this step. If you prefer, swap out the chips for crackers, pitas, or sliced crunchy vegetables.

- **Hands-On Time: 10 minutes**
- **Cook Time: 25 minutes**

Serves 1

- **4 ounces cream cheese, softened**
- **2 tablespoons mayonnaise**
- **2 tablespoons sautéed spinach**
- **2 tablespoons finely minced artichoke hearts**
- **1 tablespoon chopped green chilies**
- **½ cup shredded mozzarella cheese**
- **2 tablespoons shredded Parmesan cheese, divided**
- **⅛ teaspoon salt**
- **⅛ teaspoon crushed red pepper flakes**
- **1 cup water**

1 Grease an 8-ounce ramekin. Set aside.

2 In a small bowl, combine cream cheese, mayonnaise, spinach, artichokes, chilies, mozzarella, 1 tablespoon Parmesan, salt, and red pepper flakes. Spoon the mixture into prepared ramekin and cover with foil.

3 Pour water into Instant Pot® and add the trivet. Place ramekin on trivet.

4 Close the lid; turn the knob to Sealing.

5 Press Manual or Pressure Cook button and adjust time to 20 minutes.

6 When the timer beeps, immediately turn the knob from Sealing to Venting, then remove the lid and carefully remove ramekin to an ovenproof plate.

7 Preheat oven broiler or air fryer to high.

8 Uncover the dip and sprinkle the top with remaining 1 tablespoon Parmesan.

9 Broil 3–5 minutes until browned on top. Serve immediately.

PER SERVING

CALORIES: 824 | FAT: 68g | PROTEIN: 25g | SODIUM: 1,470mg
FIBER: 2g | CARBOHYDRATES: 14g | SUGAR: 6g

Creamy Corn Dip

This super-creamy corn dip is a little bit spicy, a little sweet, and just addicting! Feel free to use fresh, frozen, or canned corn in this dip, and serve with crusty bread, chips, crackers, or vegetables.

- **Hands-On Time: 10 minutes**
- **Cook Time: 20 minutes**

Serves 1

2 ounces cream cheese, softened
3 tablespoons shredded Cheddar cheese
1 tablespoon minced pickled jalapeño peppers
½ cup corn
1 tablespoon bacon bits
1⁄16 teaspoon salt
1⁄16 teaspoon ground black pepper
1 cup water
1 tablespoon shredded Parmesan cheese

1 Grease an 8-ounce ramekin. Set aside.

2 In a small bowl, combine cream cheese, Cheddar, jalapeños, corn, bacon bits, salt, and pepper. Spoon the mixture into prepared ramekin and cover with foil.

3 Pour water into Instant Pot® and add the trivet. Place ramekin on trivet.

4 Close the lid; turn the knob to Sealing.

5 Press Manual or Pressure Cook button and adjust time to 15 minutes.

6 When the timer beeps, immediately turn the knob from Sealing to Venting, then remove the lid and carefully remove ramekin to an ovenproof plate.

7 Preheat oven broiler or air fryer to high.

8 Uncover dip and sprinkle the top with Parmesan.

9 Broil 3–5 minutes until browned on top. Serve immediately.

PER SERVING

CALORIES: 391 | FAT: 27g | PROTEIN: 16g | SODIUM: 828mg
FIBER: 2g | CARBOHYDRATES: 16g | SUGAR: 6g

Personal Pepperoni Pizza Dip

Enjoy all the flavors of a personal pizza without the carbs! This pizza dip is creamy, rich, and cheesy—perfect for when you're craving pizza and need a quick fix. You can add any additional "toppings" to the dip that you love on your pizza.

- **Hands-On Time: 10 minutes**
- **Cook Time: 20 minutes**

Serves 1

2 ounces cream cheese, softened

3 tablespoons shredded mozzarella cheese, divided

⅛ teaspoon garlic powder

⅛ teaspoon plus 1/16 teaspoon Italian seasoning, divided

⅛ teaspoon salt

3 tablespoons marinara sauce

1 tablespoon diced pepperoni

1 teaspoon shredded Parmesan cheese

1 cup water

1 Grease an 8-ounce ramekin. Set aside.

2 In a small bowl, combine cream cheese, 2 tablespoons mozzarella, garlic powder, ⅛ teaspoon Italian seasoning, and salt. Spoon mixture into prepared ramekin.

3 Top with marinara, remaining 1 tablespoon mozzarella, pepperoni, Parmesan, and remaining 1/16 teaspoon Italian seasoning. Cover with foil.

4 Pour water into Instant Pot® and add the trivet. Place ramekin on trivet.

5 Close the lid; turn the knob to Sealing.

6 Press Manual or Pressure Cook button and adjust time to 15 minutes.

7 When the timer beeps, immediately turn the knob from Sealing to Venting, then remove the lid and carefully remove ramekin to an ovenproof plate.

8 Preheat oven broiler or air fryer to high.

9 Uncover dip and broil 3–5 minutes until browned on top. Serve immediately.

PER SERVING

CALORIES: 385 | FAT: 29g | PROTEIN: 13g | SODIUM: 1,344mg
FIBER: 2g | CARBOHYDRATES: 11g | SUGAR: 8g

Creamy Chili-Cheese Dip

I love serving this chili-cheese dip on its own with corn chips to dip, or poured over nachos, hot dogs, or even rice.

- **Hands-On Time: 10 minutes**
- **Cook Time: 25 minutes**

Serves 1

3 ounces cream cheese, softened
½ cup chili (any kind)
4 tablespoons shredded Cheddar cheese, divided
1 cup water

1 Grease an 8-ounce ramekin. Set aside.

2 In a small bowl, combine cream cheese, chili, and 3 tablespoons Cheddar. Spoon the mixture into prepared ramekin and cover with foil.

3 Pour water into Instant Pot® and add the trivet. Place ramekin on trivet.

4 Close the lid; turn the knob to Sealing.

5 Press Manual or Pressure Cook button and adjust time to 20 minutes.

6 When the timer beeps, immediately turn the knob from Sealing to Venting, then remove the lid and carefully remove ramekin to an ovenproof plate.

7 Preheat oven broiler or air fryer to high.

8 Uncover dip and sprinkle the top with remaining 1 tablespoon Cheddar.

9 Broil 3–5 minutes until browned on top. Serve immediately.

PER SERVING

CALORIES: 434 | FAT: 33g | PROTEIN: 13g | SODIUM: 496mg
FIBER: 1g | CARBOHYDRATES: 11g | SUGAR: 7g

Beef and Pork

Beef and pork give so much variety to cooking, from ribs to sausage and steak to stew meat, not to mention bacon, ham, and tenderloin. Options abound in their preparation, whether ground, shaved, or sliced. Because of the diversity of these two power proteins, you can make a wide variety of different meals with them.

For starters, ground beef and pork are two of the most affordable and accessible proteins and can be used in Cheesy Stuffed Peppers, Teriyaki-Glazed Meatloaf and Mashed Potatoes, Reverse Egg Roll Bowl, or my famous Quinoa, Beef, and Bean Lettuce Wraps. Ribs are another favorite choice when cooking for one. You can always find a small rack of ribs for less than half of what you'd pay at a restaurant, and often they're already marinated and seasoned. Pork tenderloin is an excellent option because it's usually portioned in a manageable size for cooking one meal, and it freezes nicely for when you're ready for it.

I hope these recipes inspire you to try something new and treat yourself!

Teriyaki-Glazed Meatloaf and Mashed Potatoes

My mom made meatloaf with a sweet teriyaki glaze instead of traditional ketchup, and now I can't do it any other way. I know you'll love this fun Asian twist on an American classic.

- **Hands-On Time: 15 minutes**
- **Cook Time: 25 minutes**

Serves 1

Meatloaf
½ pound 80/20 ground beef
1 teaspoon minced garlic
2 tablespoons whole milk
3 tablespoons panko bread crumbs
½ tablespoon dried onion flakes
½ teaspoon Dijon mustard
½ tablespoon soy sauce
1 large egg
⅛ teaspoon crushed red pepper flakes
⅛ teaspoon salt

Mashed Potatoes
1½ cups peeled and diced russet potatoes
1 cup chicken broth
1 tablespoon butter
3 tablespoons heavy cream
⅛ teaspoon salt

Teriyaki Glaze
2 tablespoons ketchup
2 tablespoons brown sugar
1 tablespoon soy sauce
¼ teaspoon sriracha sauce
⅛ teaspoon crushed red pepper flakes
⅛ teaspoon minced garlic

1 In a small bowl, mix together all Meatloaf ingredients until combined and press into an ungreased 6" cake pan. Set aside.

2 To make Mashed Potatoes, to the Instant Pot®, add diced potatoes and broth. Add the trivet on top of potatoes. Place prepared cake pan on top of the trivet.

3 Close the lid; turn the knob to Sealing.

4 Press Manual or Pressure Cook button and adjust time to 20 minutes. While meatloaf is cooking, make the glaze.

5 In a small saucepan over medium heat, mix together all Teriyaki Glaze ingredients about 5 minutes until bubbly and thick. Set aside.

6 When the timer beeps, immediately turn the knob from Sealing to Venting, then remove the lid.

7 Carefully remove meatloaf and trivet and set aside. Drain potatoes, then remove to a small bowl. Add butter, cream, and salt. Using a fork or potato masher, mash potatoes until they reach the desired consistency.

8 Remove meatloaf from pan. Arrange potatoes on a serving plate with meatloaf. Spoon the Teriyaki Glaze over meatloaf and serve.

PER SERVING

CALORIES: 1,348 | FAT: 71g | PROTEIN: 58g | SODIUM: 3,522mg
FIBER: 3g | CARBOHYDRATES: 100g | SUGAR: 43g

Cheesy Stuffed Peppers

This recipe is an awesome and easy way to use up rice left over from any of the rice recipes in Chapter 10, or to make as a healthy and hearty dinner.

- **Hands-On Time: 8 minutes**
- **Cook Time: 15 minutes**

Serves 1

¼ cup 80/20 ground beef

¼ cup cooked brown rice

½ teaspoon soy sauce

½ teaspoon minced garlic

¼ teaspoon Italian seasoning

4 tablespoons tomato sauce, divided

⅛ teaspoon granulated beef bouillon

4 tablespoons shredded Cheddar cheese, divided

1½ tablespoons minced mushrooms

½ teaspoon dried onion flakes

⅛ teaspoon salt

1 large green bell pepper, top removed, seeded, and cored

1 cup water

1 In a small bowl, combine beef, rice, soy sauce, garlic, Italian seasoning, 1 table-spoon tomato sauce, bouillon, 2 tablespoons Cheddar, mushrooms, onion flakes, and salt. Scoop mixture into hollowed-out bell pepper.

2 Top filling with 1 tablespoon tomato sauce and remaining 2 tablespoons Cheddar.

3 Pour water into Instant Pot® and add the trivet. Place bell pepper on trivet.

4 Close the lid; turn the knob to Sealing.

5 Press Manual or Pressure Cook button and adjust time to 15 minutes.

6 When the timer beeps, immediately turn the knob from Sealing to Venting, then remove the lid.

7 Using tongs, carefully remove pepper to a plate and top with remaining 2 tablespoons tomato sauce. Let stand 5 minutes, then serve.

PER SERVING

CALORIES: 365 | **FAT:** 19g | **PROTEIN:** 21g | **SODIUM:** 1,207mg
FIBER: 5g | **CARBOHYDRATES:** 24g | **SUGAR:** 7g

Reverse Egg Roll Bowl

I don't know about you, but I *love* a yummy, crispy egg roll slathered in a sweet chili sauce. However, I don't love the idea of eating so much of the carb-laden wrapper with so little filling. This one-pot dish solves all my problems! I get all the goodness of the low-carb filling topped with the perfect amount of crunch on top. Of course, it's all still slathered in sauce! If you can't find crispy wonton strips, try using chow mein noodles.

- Hands-On Time: 2 minutes
- Cook Time: 6 minutes

Serves 1

1 tablespoon sesame oil
¾ cup ground pork
1 teaspoon grated fresh ginger
½ teaspoon minced garlic
1½ teaspoons soy sauce
¼ teaspoon sriracha sauce
¼ teaspoon hoisin sauce
½ tablespoon dried
  onion flakes
¼ teaspoon salt
½ cup chicken broth
3 cups coleslaw mix
½ cup crispy wonton strips
2 tablespoons sweet
  chili sauce

1 On the Instant Pot®, press Sauté button and adjust to High.

2 Add oil, pork, ginger, garlic, soy sauce, sriracha, hoisin sauce, onion flakes, and salt. Sauté about 5 minutes until pork is cooked through and crumbly.

3 Pour in broth and coleslaw and stir to mix. Press Cancel button to turn off the heat.

4 Close the lid; turn the knob to Sealing.

5 Press Manual or Pressure Cook button and adjust time to 1 minute.

6 When the timer beeps, immediately turn the knob from Sealing to Venting, then remove the lid and transfer mixture to a serving bowl. Top with wonton strips and chili sauce. Serve.

PER SERVING

CALORIES: 771 | FAT: 44g | PROTEIN: 39g | SODIUM: 2,256mg
FIBER: 5g | CARBOHYDRATES: 49g | SUGAR: 2g

Cajun Dirty Rice with Andouille Sausage

This hearty dish is packed with flavors and vegetables! It's perfect to make as a single portion to use up any leftover vegetables or meat that may otherwise go to waste. Throw it all in the Instant Pot® together, and you've got a delicious one-pot meal.

- **Hands-On Time: 5 minutes**
- **Cook Time: 16 minutes**

Serves 1

1 tablespoon olive oil

1 tablespoon finely minced yellow onion

¼ cup diced red and green bell pepper

2 tablespoons finely minced celery

1½ cups sliced andouille sausage

½ teaspoon minced garlic

½ teaspoon Cajun seasoning

⅛ teaspoon dried thyme

⅛ teaspoon smoked paprika

⅛ teaspoon dried oregano

½ tablespoon soy sauce

1 cup chicken broth

½ cup uncooked long-grain white rice

½ tablespoon chopped fresh parsley

1 On the Instant Pot®, press Sauté button and adjust to High.

2 Add oil, onion, bell pepper, celery, sausage, and garlic. Sauté 3 minutes.

3 Add Cajun seasoning, thyme, paprika, oregano, soy sauce, and broth. Deglaze the pot, scraping all the browned bits off the bottom of the pot. Press Cancel button to turn off the heat, then stir in rice.

4 Close the lid; turn the knob to Sealing.

5 Press Manual or Pressure Cook button and adjust time to 3 minutes.

6 When the timer beeps, allow 10 minutes to naturally release the pressure, then remove the lid.

7 Spoon the mixture into a bowl, top with parsley, and serve.

PER SERVING

CALORIES: 1,229 | FAT: 72g | PROTEIN: 66g | SODIUM: 5,464mg
FIBER: 11g | CARBOHYDRATES: 87g | SUGAR: 3g

Creamy Spicy Italian Sausage and Spaghetti Squash "Pasta"

This low-carb take on angel hair Alfredo is the perfect way to use up half of a Steamed Spaghetti Squash (see Chapter 4).

- **Hands-On Time: 5 minutes**
- **Cook Time: 33 minutes**

Serves 1

1 cup water
1 small spaghetti squash
1 cup ground Italian sausage
1 teaspoon minced garlic
¼ teaspoon crushed red pepper flakes
⅛ teaspoon salt
½ cup chicken broth
½ cup heavy cream
¼ cup shredded Parmesan cheese
1 cup packed spinach

SPAGHETTI SQUASH TIPS

When properly cooked, spaghetti squash strands will be tender and not crunchy. Since the hardness of the squash greatly depends on the size and how old it is (the water content), you may need to add additional cooking time if the squash is not completely cooked after the initial pressure cook. When you can easily pierce a knife into the squash, you'll know it's ready to eat.

1 Pour water into Instant Pot® and add the trivet. Place spaghetti squash on trivet.

2 Close the lid; turn the knob to Sealing.

3 Press Manual or Pressure Cook button and adjust time to 25 minutes.

4 When the timer beeps, turn the knob from Sealing to Venting, remove the lid, and transfer squash to a cutting board.

5 Slice squash in half. (Cutting squash through the stem will result in shorter strands, while cutting crosswise through the middle will result in longer strands.) Scoop out seeds from each half and discard. Using tongs or a fork, gently scrape and pull the squash strands out of the shell into a strainer. Push the squash against the sides of the strainer to remove as much liquid as possible, then measure 1 packed cup for this dish and reserve the rest for another use.

6 Drain and rinse out the Instant Pot® liner. Press Sauté button and adjust to High.

7 Add sausage, garlic, red pepper flakes, and salt. Sauté about 5–8 minutes until sausage is cooked through. Add broth, cream, and Parmesan. Deglaze the pot, scraping all the browned bits off the bottom of the pot.

8 Add spinach and squash, then toss everything to coat until the spinach is wilted, about 2 minutes. Transfer to a serving bowl and serve immediately.

PER SERVING

CALORIES: 1,426 | FAT: 116g | PROTEIN: 48g | SODIUM: 2,907mg
FIBER: 7g | CARBOHYDRATES: 37g | SUGAR: 15g

Italian Sausage and Vegetables

This easy one-pot meal is great for busy nights, since everything cooks so quickly and there are few ingredients. There are many different varieties of sausage, so choose your favorite!

- **Hands-On Time: 3 minutes**
- **Cook Time: 2 minutes**

Serves 1

½ tablespoon butter

2 links Italian sausage, sliced into ½" pieces

½ cup sliced green bell pepper

½ cup sliced red bell pepper

¾ cup sliced zucchini

½ cup chicken broth

1 teaspoon Italian seasoning

1 teaspoon ground lemon pepper

1 To the Instant Pot®, add all ingredients.

2 Close the lid; turn the knob to Sealing.

3 Press Manual or Pressure Cook button and adjust time to 2 minutes.

4 When the timer beeps, immediately turn the knob from Sealing to Venting, then remove the lid and carefully transfer the sausages and vegetables to a serving plate. Serve.

PER SERVING

CALORIES: 665 | **FAT:** 49g | **PROTEIN:** 34g | **SODIUM:** 2,592mg **FIBER:** 3g | **CARBOHYDRATES:** 15g | **SUGAR:** 7g

Sausage, Green Bean, and Potato Boil

This is the land version of a seafood boil. Spicy sausage, tender potatoes, and crisp green beans combine and cook all together to make a super-easy, quick, and satisfying dinner. Serve with additional Old Bay seasoning, if desired.

- **Hands-On Time: 1 minute**
- **Cook Time: 10 minutes**

Serves 1

½ tablespoon butter

6 ounces fresh green beans, trimmed

2 links Cajun-style sausage, sliced

1 medium unpeeled red potato, cut into 1" pieces

½ cup chicken broth

1 teaspoon Old Bay seasoning

1 In the Instant Pot®, combine all ingredients.

2 Close the lid; turn the knob to Sealing.

3 Press Manual or Pressure Cook button and adjust time to 5 minutes.

4 When the timer beeps, allow 5 minutes to naturally release the pressure, then remove the lid.

5 Transfer to a serving bowl and serve.

PER SERVING

CALORIES: 578 | **FAT:** 30g | **PROTEIN:** 32g | **SODIUM:** 2,389mg **FIBER:** 8g | **CARBOHYDRATES:** 50g | **SUGAR:** 9g

Mushroom-Beef Stroganoff Sauce

Tender pieces of beef and mushroom combine for a creamy, thick sauce that is simply comfort in a bowl. I like to mix it up and serve with mashed potatoes, egg noodles, or spaghetti squash (for a low-carb option!).

- **Hands-On Time: 2 minutes**
- **Cook Time: 48 minutes**

Serves 1

1 tablespoon butter
1 cup beef stew meat
¼ teaspoon salt
¼ teaspoon ground
    black pepper
¼ teaspoon smoked paprika
½ teaspoon dried thyme
1½ cups mushrooms
1 teaspoon dried onion flakes
½ teaspoon minced garlic
1 teaspoon soy sauce
1 cup beef broth
1 tablespoon cornstarch
1 tablespoon cold water
¼ cup sour cream

1 On the Instant Pot®, press Sauté button and adjust to High.

2 Add butter and cook about 2 minutes until browned slightly. In a small bowl, sprinkle meat with salt, pepper, paprika, and thyme. Add meat to the Instant Pot® and sear 3 minutes per side. Do not stir while searing.

3 Add mushrooms, onion flakes, garlic, soy sauce, and broth. Deglaze the pot, scraping all the browned bits off the bottom of the pot. Press Cancel button to turn off the heat.

4 Close the lid; turn the knob to Sealing.

5 Press Manual or Pressure Cook button and adjust time to 30 minutes.

6 When the timer beeps, allow 10 minutes to naturally release the pressure, then remove the lid.

7 Press Sauté button and adjust to High. Bring mixture to a boil.

8 In a small bowl, whisk together cornstarch and water. Whisk cornstarch mixture into the sauce to thicken. Stir in sour cream and transfer to a bowl. Serve immediately.

PER SERVING

CALORIES: 581 | FAT: 32g | PROTEIN: 57g | SODIUM: 1,978mg
FIBER: 2g | CARBOHYDRATES: 16g | SUGAR: 4g

Quinoa, Beef, and Bean Lettuce Wraps

This recipe is easy, healthy, and ready in 20 minutes or less from prep to table. Scoop this filling into a lettuce wrap or tortilla for a delicious and quick meal. I've also had success using ground turkey in this recipe. The taco seasoning can be adjusted to your individual taste.

- **Hands-On Time: 5 minutes**
- **Cook Time: 12 minutes**

Serves 1

¼ pound 80/20 ground beef

¼ cup uncooked quinoa, rinsed

⅓ cup drained and rinsed canned black beans

1 tablespoon taco seasoning, divided

1 tablespoon chopped green chilies

½ cup beef broth

For Serving

4 leaves iceberg lettuce

¼ cup diced avocado

2 tablespoons diced tomato

2 tablespoons sour cream

2 tablespoons salsa

2 tablespoons shredded Cheddar cheese

1 tablespoon chopped cilantro

1 On the Instant Pot®, press Sauté button and adjust to High. Add beef and sauté about 5 minutes until cooked. Add quinoa, beans, ½ tablespoon taco seasoning, chilies, and broth. Deglaze the pot, scraping all the browned bits off the bottom of the pot. Press Cancel button to turn off the heat.

2 Close the lid; turn the knob to Sealing.

3 Press Manual or Pressure Cook button and adjust time to 2 minutes.

4 When the timer beeps, allow 5 minutes to naturally release the pressure, then remove the lid.

5 Fluff beef mixture and add remaining ½ tablespoon taco seasoning.

6 Line a bowl with lettuce leaves. Scoop mixture into the bowl and top with remaining toppings. Serve.

PER SERVING

CALORIES: 770 | **FAT:** 38g | **PROTEIN:** 38g | **SODIUM:** 1,706mg
FIBER: 16g | **CARBOHYDRATES:** 56g | **SUGAR:** 6g

The Best Instant Pot® Ribs

These ribs are on my website, and they always get the best feedback! The great part is that you may substitute ½ cup of your favorite dry rub blend for my dry rub recipe. Look for the smallest rack of ribs you can find, or cut a larger rack into two portions—eat one now, freeze the other for later.

- **Hands-On Time: 15 minutes**
- **Cook Time: 58 minutes**

Serves 1

1 (3–4 pound) rack pork ribs, back membrane removed
½ cup barbecue sauce

Dry Rub
¼ cup brown sugar
2 tablespoons smoked paprika
1 tablespoon kosher salt
1 tablespoon chili powder
1 tablespoon onion powder
1 tablespoon garlic powder

Liquid Ingredients
1 cup apple juice
1 tablespoon apple cider vinegar
1 tablespoon soy sauce
½ tablespoon liquid smoke

HOW TO REMOVE BACK MEMBRANE

Ribs have a shiny membrane on the backside of the bones. Before cooking, flip the ribs over to the back and lift up a corner of the membrane with a dry paper towel. Grasp it firmly and pull up to remove.

1 Cut rack of ribs into two portions and place in a gallon-sized zip-top bag. Add Dry Rub and Liquid Ingredients and massage marinade all over ribs. Squeeze out all of the air from bag and refrigerate at least 8 hours or up to 2 days.

2 Add the trivet to the Instant Pot® and pour entire bag of ribs and marinade into the pot.

3 Close the lid; turn the knob to Sealing.

4 Press Manual or Pressure Cook button and adjust time to 40 minutes.

5 When the timer beeps, allow 10 minutes to naturally release the pressure, then remove the lid.

6 Preheat oven broiler to high. Line a baking sheet with foil.

7 Remove ribs to prepared baking sheet. Pour barbecue sauce over ribs and brush evenly to coat. Broil 5–8 minutes until browned and caramelized. Transfer to a plate and serve.

PER SERVING

CALORIES: 2,876 | FAT: 171g | PROTEIN: 184g | SODIUM: 5,748mg
FIBER: 6g | CARBOHYDRATES: 100g | SUGAR: 78g

Four-Ingredient Country-Style Ribs

Country Style Ribs actually aren't "ribs" at all, but they're a perfect portion for individual cooking! This is such an easy recipe, because you basically just dump everything into the pot and you're ready to go! You can make as many ribs as you like, and the cook time will stay the same.

- **Hands-On Time: 5 minutes**
- **Cook Time: 50 minutes**

Serves 1

4 pieces (about 12 ounces)
    boneless country-style ribs
2 tablespoons barbecue dry
    rub
¾ cup barbecue sauce,
    divided
½ cup root beer, cola, or
    other dark-colored soda

TIP

Mix up the ingredients to your taste and experiment with different flavors of dry rub, sauce, and soda or liquid. For example, I like to combine garlic, salt, and black pepper and use a teriyaki or hoisin-based sauce with a soy sauce–spiked cooking liquid for an Asian-inspired preparation.

1   To the Instant Pot®, add ribs, rub, ½ cup barbecue sauce, and root beer or other soda. Toss to coat the ribs.

2   Close the lid; turn the knob to Sealing.

3   Press Manual or Pressure Cook button and adjust time to 35 minutes.

4   When the timer beeps, allow 15 minutes to naturally release the pressure, then remove the lid.

5   Remove ribs to a serving plate and baste with remaining ¼ cup barbecue sauce. If desired, broil ribs under a preheated oven broiler 5 minutes until caramelized.

PER SERVING

CALORIES: 1,420 | FAT: 56g | PROTEIN: 93g | SODIUM: 3,557mg
FIBER: 8g | CARBOHYDRATES: 110g | SUGAR: 84g

Japanese Beef Curry

Potatoes, carrots, and onions are staples in this dish, but you can add any other vegetables that you like, such as sweet potatoes, green beans, corn, and so on. The possibilities are endless. I often make this meal using leftover pot roast.

- **Hands-On Time: 5 minutes**
- **Cook Time: 65 minutes**

Serves 1

1 tablespoon olive oil

1 cup diced stew meat in bite-sized pieces

¼ teaspoon salt

¼ teaspoon ground black pepper

½ medium yellow onion, peeled and sliced

½ cup baby carrots

1 cup peeled and diced russet potatoes

2 cups water

1 tablespoon ketchup

1 tablespoon soy sauce

½ tablespoon cocoa powder

1 (3.5-ounce) box dry Japanese curry sauce mix

1 cup cooked white sticky rice

WHAT IS JAPANESE CURRY?
Unlike Indian or Thai curry, Japanese curry has a dark, deeper flavor that varies in spiciness. It's much more understated and can carry a sweeter taste. Look for curry sauce mix in the international food aisle of your local grocery store. Depending on the spiciness level, I start with half the package and add more to taste.

1 On the Instant Pot®, press Sauté button and adjust to High. Add oil. In a small bowl, season stew meat with salt and pepper.

2 When oil is hot and shiny, add meat to the Instant Pot® in a single layer and do not stir. Allow to sear 5 minutes on one side, then flip and sear the other side. Push meat to one side of the Instant Pot® and add onion. Sauté 5 minutes.

3 Add carrots, potatoes, water, ketchup, soy sauce, and cocoa powder and stir. Press Cancel button to turn off the heat.

4 Close the lid; turn the knob to Sealing.

5 Press Manual or Pressure Cook button and adjust time to 30 minutes.

6 When the timer beeps, allow 15 minutes to naturally release the pressure, then remove the lid.

7 Stir in curry sauce mix about 5 minutes until completely dissolved. Transfer to a plate and serve with rice.

PER SERVING

CALORIES: 1,301 | FAT: 53g | PROTEIN: 64g | SODIUM: 6,266mg FIBER: 13g | CARBOHYDRATES: 135g | SUGAR: 20g

Fall-Apart Beef Short Ribs and Gravy

Beef short ribs are such a treat! They're usually found in small packages, which is an economical way to cook a fancy meal for one. These short ribs are incredibly tender, with a thick, dark sauce that will have you licking the plate!

- **Hands-On Time: 25 minutes**
- **Cook Time: 90 minutes**

Serves 1

1 tablespoon olive oil
4 pieces (about 1½ pounds) beef short ribs
¼ teaspoon ground black pepper
¼ teaspoon garlic salt
⅛ teaspoon garlic powder
⅛ teaspoon smoked paprika
½ cup beef broth
⅛ teaspoon Dijon mustard
¼ teaspoon balsamic vinegar
1 teaspoon soy sauce
⅛ teaspoon dried rosemary

1. On the Instant Pot®, press Sauté button and adjust to High. Add oil.

2. Wash ribs under cool running water to remove any bone fragments, then pat dry. In a small bowl, mix together pepper, garlic salt, garlic powder, and paprika. Sprinkle evenly over ribs.

3. When oil is shiny and hot, sear ribs 5 minutes per side without stirring so you get the darkest, best sear possible. Press Cancel button to turn off the heat.

4. Add broth, mustard, vinegar, soy sauce, and rosemary. Deglaze the pot, scraping all the browned bits off the bottom of the pot.

5. Close the lid; turn the knob to Sealing.

6. Press Manual or Pressure Cook button and adjust time to 50 minutes.

7. When the timer beeps, allow a full natural pressure release until the pin drops, about 20 minutes, then remove the lid.

8. Transfer ribs to a serving plate and cover with foil. On the Instant Pot®, press Sauté button and adjust to High. Cook remaining liquid about 10 minutes until it's reduced and coats the back of a spoon. Pour sauce over ribs and serve.

PER SERVING

CALORIES: 668 | FAT: 43g | PROTEIN: 58g | SODIUM: 1,347mg
FIBER: 0g | CARBOHYDRATES: 1g | SUGAR: 0g

Mushroom Pork Tenderloin with Mashed Potatoes and Gravy

This sumptuous dish quickly cooks pork tenderloin and mashed potatoes at the same time while keeping them separate.

- **Hands-On Time: 5 minutes**
- **Cook Time: 47 minutes**

Serves 1

Pork
¼ teaspoon garlic powder
¼ teaspoon salt
¼ teaspoon smoked paprika
¼ teaspoon Italian seasoning
¼ teaspoon ground
   black pepper
¼ teaspoon dried rosemary
½ teaspoon dried basil
½ pound pork tenderloin
1 tablespoon olive oil
½ cup sliced mushrooms
1 cup chicken broth
½ teaspoon minced garlic
1 teaspoon soy sauce
1 tablespoon cornstarch
1 tablespoon cold water

Potatoes
1½ cups peeled and diced
   russet potatoes in ½" pieces
2 tablespoons butter
1½ tablespoons whole milk
⅛ teaspoon salt

1. In a small bowl, mix together garlic powder, salt, paprika, Italian seasoning, pepper, rosemary, and basil. Pat all over pork tenderloin.

2. On the Instant Pot®, press Sauté button and adjust to High. Add oil. When hot and shiny, add pork and mushrooms and sear 5 minutes each side. Press Cancel button to turn off the heat.

3. Add broth, garlic, and soy sauce. Deglaze the pot, scraping all the browned bits off the bottom of the pot.

4. Pour potatoes into a 6" cake pan.

5. Add the trivet over pork and place cake pan on top of the trivet.

6. Close the lid; turn the knob to Sealing.

7. Press Manual or Pressure Cook button and adjust time to 25 minutes.

8. When the timer beeps, allow 10 minutes to naturally release the pressure, then remove the lid and press Sauté button.

9. Carefully remove the pan of potatoes and trivet. Transfer potatoes to a small bowl and add butter, milk, and salt. Mash to desired consistency and scoop onto a serving plate. Remove pork to a serving plate.

10. In a cup, stir together cornstarch and water. Slowly whisk into the hot juices in the pot and cook about 2 minutes until thickened. Spoon gravy over pork and potatoes and serve.

PER SERVING

CALORIES: 838 | **FAT:** 43g | **PROTEIN:** 57g | **SODIUM:** 2,628mg
FIBER: 4g | **CARBOHYDRATES:** 53g | **SUGAR:** 6g

Ham and Potato Au Gratin

This warm and cheesy dish is an amazing way to make a filling meal with one potato and some diced ham. If you don't want to use ham, you can mix it up with whatever precooked protein you have on hand, which makes it incredibly versatile when cooking for one.

- **Hands-On Time: 20 minutes**
- **Cook Time: 87 minutes**

Serves 1

1 cup water
1 tablespoon butter
1 tablespoon all-purpose flour
¾ cup whole milk
1¼ cups shredded Cheddar cheese, divided
⅛ teaspoon ground black pepper
⅛ teaspoon salt
1 medium unpeeled russet potato, sliced into ⅛" circles
½ cup diced ham

HOW TO KEEP POTATOES FROM TURNING BROWN

If you slice your potatoes ahead of making the cheese sauce, make sure to keep them submerged in cool water to prevent the potatoes from turning red or brown. When you're ready to start assembling your dish, drain the potatoes and shake off any excess water, and they'll be ready to use.

1 Grease a 6" cake pan. Set aside.

2 Pour water into Instant Pot® and add the trivet.

3 In a small saucepan over medium heat, melt butter and whisk in flour to make a roux. Cook 1 minute, then slowly add milk, whisking constantly.

4 Turn off heat and slowly whisk in ½ cup Cheddar. Whisk in pepper and salt and set aside.

5 To prepared cake pan, add 2 tablespoons cheese sauce. Add six potato slices in a layer on top of sauce, then top with 2 tablespoons each ham, Cheddar, and cheese sauce. Repeat layers until all potato slices have been used. Top the last layer with remaining sauce and Cheddar and cover the pan with foil.

6 Place pan on trivet.

7 Close the lid; turn the knob to Sealing.

8 Press Manual or Pressure Cook button and adjust time to 85 minutes.

9 When the timer beeps, immediately turn the knob from Sealing to Venting, then remove the lid and carefully remove pan. Let stand 10 minutes. Serve, or, if desired, remove the foil and broil 5 minutes under a preheated oven broiler or air fryer.

PER SERVING

CALORIES: 1,095 | FAT: 63g | PROTEIN: 61g | SODIUM: 2,271mg
FIBER: 4g | CARBOHYDRATES: 54g | SUGAR: 12g

Alfredo Cheese Tortellini with Bacon and Peas

You may use fresh or frozen tortellini for this simple yet flavor-packed dish. Try experimenting with your favorite filled pastas to mix up the flavors.

- **Hands-On Time: 5 minutes**
- **Cook Time: 10 minutes**

Serves 1

1½ cups uncooked
    cheese tortellini
¾ cup chicken broth
1 cup heavy cream
½ teaspoon minced garlic
½ cup cooked and chopped
    thick-cut bacon
½ cup frozen peas
½ cup shredded
    Parmesan cheese

1 To the Instant Pot®, add tortellini, broth, cream, garlic, and bacon. Do not stir.

2 Close the lid; turn the knob to Sealing.

3 Press Manual or Pressure Cook button and adjust time to 5 minutes.

4 When the timer beeps, allow 5 minutes to naturally release the pressure, then remove the lid.

5 Stir in peas, then Parmesan. Transfer to a bowl and serve.

PER SERVING

CALORIES: 1,978 | FAT: 135g | PROTEIN: 78g | SODIUM: 3,738mg
FIBER: 6g | CARBOHYDRATES: 96g | SUGAR: 13g

Citrusy Pork Carnitas

Delicious pork tenderloin rubbed in smoky spices cooks in orange and lime juices for the ultimate pork carnitas. You can stuff this pork into a taco or burrito, or serve it with rice, on top of a salad, or just by itself!

- **Hands-On Time: 10 minutes**
- **Cook Time: 33 minutes**

Serves 1

2 tablespoons olive oil, divided
½ pound pork tenderloin, chopped into 4 pieces
½ teaspoon Italian seasoning
¼ teaspoon garlic powder
¼ teaspoon chili powder
¼ teaspoon salt
¼ teaspoon dried oregano
⅛ teaspoon smoked paprika
⅛ teaspoon ground lemon pepper
½ cup orange juice
1 tablespoon lime juice
1 teaspoon soy sauce

1 On the Instant Pot®, press Sauté button and adjust to High. Add 1 tablespoon oil.

2 In a small bowl, mix together remaining 1 tablespoon oil, pork, Italian seasoning, garlic powder, chili powder, salt, oregano, paprika, and lemon pepper. Toss to coat completely.

3 Add meat to Instant Pot® and sear each piece 4 minutes a side. Press Cancel button to turn off the heat.

4 To the Instant Pot®, add orange juice, lime juice, and soy sauce. Deglaze the pot, scraping all the browned bits off the bottom of the pot.

5 Close the lid; turn the knob to Sealing.

6 Press Manual or Pressure Cook button and adjust time to 15 minutes.

7 When the timer beeps, allow 10 minutes to naturally release the pressure, then remove the lid.

8 Using two forks, shred meat. Transfer to a serving plate and serve.

PER SERVING

CALORIES: 565 | **FAT:** 33g | **PROTEIN:** 47g | **SODIUM:** 1,450mg
FIBER: 1g | **CARBOHYDRATES:** 17g | **SUGAR:** 11g

Lazy Shabu Shabu Bowl

Shabu shabu is essentially a Japanese fondue. You quickly swish thinly cut slices of meat, noodles, and vegetables in broth and dip in a citrusy ponzu or creamy sesame sauce. It may be impractical to arrange this for one, so try doing it the "lazy" way by cooking it all in the Instant Pot® at once. The best part is that you can add all your favorite ingredients and use water or broth.

- **Hands-On Time: 2 minutes**
- **Cook Time: 1 minute**

Serves 1

1 cup dashi broth

2 cups chopped napa cabbage

1 cup assorted mushrooms (shiitake, enoki, beech, and seafood)

1 medium green onion, chopped

1 (6–8-ounce) block frozen udon noodles

1 cup thinly sliced frozen pork

½ cup ponzu sauce

½ cup sesame sauce

1 To the Instant Pot®, add broth, cabbage, mushrooms, and green onion. Place noodles and pork on top of vegetables.

2 Close the lid; turn the knob to Sealing.

3 Press Manual or Pressure Cook button and adjust time to 1 minute.

4 When the timer beeps, immediately turn the knob from Sealing to Venting, then remove the lid.

5 Strain the contents of the pot in a colander or use tongs to transfer to a serving bowl. Serve with ponzu sauce and sesame sauce to dip.

PER SERVING

CALORIES: 1,800 | FAT: 82g | PROTEIN: 87g | SODIUM: 4,507mg
FIBER: 9g | CARBOHYDRATES: 186g | SUGAR: 26g

7

Chicken

Chicken cooks very quickly in the Instant Pot®, even when frozen, which makes these dishes ideal for weeknight cooking. If you want to swap out a chicken breast for a bone-in chicken thigh, follow the recipe and adjust the cooking time to one from a chicken breast recipe, and vice versa. It's very adaptable and easy to use almost any type of chicken for any recipe in this chapter. For safety, chicken should be cooked to an internal temperature of 165°F if you're experimenting with different cook times.

If you're looking for a one-pot meal, I recommend my Greek Chicken Rice Bowl with Tzatziki Sauce, Easy Teriyaki Chicken Thighs and Rice, or the Cajun Chicken Pasta. I've made The Absolute Best Chicken Salad for lunch more than any other recipe in this book, and the Sweet Chili Chicken Drumsticks are one of the most affordable meals you can make (less than $2 per serving!).

Garlicky Whole Lemon Chicken Thighs and Rice

If you *love* lemon, you'll be making this easy and inexpensive dish all the time. Chicken thighs can easily be found in smaller portions and quantities in the grocery store (or ask your butcher), but you can also swap them out for a thinly cut chicken breast or tenderloins. I like serving this meal with a side of steamed broccoli or roasted vegetables.

- **Hands-On Time: 5 minutes**
- **Cook Time: 25 minutes**

Serves 1

1 tablespoon olive oil
1 tablespoon butter
2 (4-ounce) boneless, skinless chicken thighs
1 teaspoon ground lemon pepper
Juice and zest of 1 medium lemon
1 cup chicken broth
½ cup uncooked long-grain white rice
1 teaspoon Italian seasoning
1 teaspoon minced garlic
¼ teaspoon salt
⅛ teaspoon ground black pepper
1 tablespoon chopped parsley

1 On the Instant Pot®, press Sauté button and adjust to High. Add oil and butter.

2 Season chicken on all sides with lemon pepper, then sauté about 5 minutes on each side until browned. Press Cancel button to turn off the heat and remove chicken.

3 Add lemon juice and zest, and broth. Deglaze the pot, scraping all the browned bits off the bottom of the pot. Add rice, Italian seasoning, garlic, salt, and pepper. Return chicken to the Instant Pot®.

4 Close the lid; turn the knob to Sealing.

5 Press Manual or Pressure Cook button and adjust time to 10 minutes.

6 When the timer beeps, allow 5 minutes to naturally release the pressure, then remove the lid.

7 Scoop chicken and rice into a bowl, then sprinkle with parsley and serve immediately.

PER SERVING

CALORIES: 796 | FAT: 34g | PROTEIN: 36g | SODIUM: 1,593mg
FIBER: 2g | CARBOHYDRATES: 79g | SUGAR: 2g

Easy Teriyaki Chicken Thighs and Rice

Tender chicken thighs and white rice cook together in the Instant Pot® with premade teriyaki sauce for the simplest, easiest one-pot meal. With only a few ingredients, anyone can make themselves a delicious and quick meal at home. For the teriyaki sauce in this recipe, try Soy Vay Veri Veri Teriyaki Sauce. It has a thin consistency that pressure cooks well without burning.

- **Hands-On Time: 5 minutes**
- **Cook Time: 20 minutes**

Serves 1

2 (8-ounce) boneless, skinless chicken thighs
½ cup teriyaki sauce
½ cup uncooked long-grain white rice
½ cup water
½ tablespoon sesame seeds
½ tablespoon chopped green onion

1 To the Instant Pot®, add chicken and pour teriyaki sauce over the top. Place the trivet on top of chicken.

2 In a 6" cake pan, combine rice and water. Place uncovered pan on trivet.

3 Close the lid; turn the knob to Sealing.

4 Press Manual or Pressure Cook button and adjust time to 10 minutes.

5 When the timer beeps, allow 5 minutes to naturally release the pressure, then remove the lid. Press Sauté button and adjust to High.

6 Carefully remove pan from the Instant Pot® and fluff rice with a fork. Place chicken (leave teriyaki sauce in Instant Pot®) on top of rice and set aside. Cover to keep warm.

7 Cook down remaining teriyaki sauce about 5 minutes until reduced and thickened. Pour over chicken and rice, then top with sesame seeds and green onion. Serve.

PER SERVING

CALORIES: 704 | **FAT:** 12g | **PROTEIN:** 43g | **SODIUM:** 5,605mg
FIBER: 2g | **CARBOHYDRATES:** 98g | **SUGAR:** 21g

Buffalo Chicken Lettuce Wraps

Spicy, creamy, crunchy, and refreshing! This is one of my favorite quick and easy meals that I pull together for myself while I prepare my kids' lunches because it cooks super quickly and it's ready for me as soon as I'm ready to eat!

- **Hands-On Time: 5 minutes**
- **Cook Time: 15 minutes**

Serves 1

1 (8-ounce) boneless, skinless chicken breast, thinly sliced

1 cup water

$\frac{1}{16}$ teaspoon salt

$\frac{1}{16}$ teaspoon ground black pepper

1 teaspoon dry ranch seasoning

3 tablespoons buffalo sauce

1 tablespoon melted butter

$\frac{1}{2}$ tablespoon chopped green onion

2–4 leaves romaine lettuce

2 tablespoons shredded carrot

2 tablespoons crispy chow mein noodles

2 tablespoons sweetened dried cranberries

2 tablespoons ranch dressing

1. To the Instant Pot®, add chicken and water. Season chicken with salt and pepper.

2. Close the lid; turn the knob to Sealing.

3. Press Manual or Pressure Cook button and adjust time to 10 minutes.

4. When the timer beeps, allow 5 minutes to naturally release the pressure, then remove the lid.

5. Remove chicken to a small bowl and add 1 tablespoon cooking liquid. Using two forks, shred the chicken.

6. Add dry ranch seasoning, buffalo sauce, butter, and green onion. Mix thoroughly.

7. Lay lettuce leaves on a serving plate. Divide chicken mixture evenly between the lettuce leaves and top evenly with carrot, chow mein noodles, cranberries, and ranch dressing. Serve immediately.

PER SERVING

CALORIES: 565 | FAT: 30g | PROTEIN: 48g | SODIUM: 2,498mg
FIBER: 3g | CARBOHYDRATES: 26g | SUGAR: 13g

Loaded Barbecue Chicken Bowl

This hearty one-pot meal is equal parts carbs and salad, so you're getting the best of both worlds—rich and savory, plus fresh and crunchy. This is a great meal to make if you happen to have some leftover lettuce or a small side salad.

- **Hands-On Time: 5 minutes**
- **Cook Time: 23 minutes**

Serves 1

1 tablespoon olive oil

2 (4-ounce) boneless, skinless chicken thighs

1 teaspoon barbecue dry rub

¾ cup chicken broth

¼ cup uncooked long-grain white rice

¼ cup drained and rinsed canned black beans

¼ cup corn

2 tablespoons shredded Cheddar cheese

2 tablespoons barbecue sauce

½ cup shredded lettuce

¼ cup diced avocado

2 tablespoons diced cherry tomatoes

1 tablespoon diced red onion

1 tablespoon chopped cilantro

½ medium lime

1 On the Instant Pot®, press Sauté button and adjust to High. Add oil.

2 Season chicken with dry rub on all sides, then place in the Instant Pot®. Cook about 4 minutes per side until browned.

3 Remove chicken and press Cancel button to turn off the heat. Add broth and deglaze the pot, scraping all the browned bits off the bottom of the pot. Add rice, beans, and corn; return chicken to Instant Pot®. Stir.

4 Close the lid; turn the knob to Sealing.

5 Press Manual or Pressure Cook button and adjust time to 10 minutes.

6 When the timer beeps, allow 5 minutes to naturally release the pressure, then remove the lid.

7 Scoop chicken mixture into a serving bowl, then top with Cheddar, barbecue sauce, lettuce, avocado, tomatoes, onion, cilantro, and lime. Serve.

PER SERVING

CALORIES: 832 | FAT: 36g | PROTEIN: 42g | SODIUM: 1,590mg
FIBER: 12g | CARBOHYDRATES: 78g | SUGAR: 16g

Sweet Chili Chicken Drumsticks

Chicken legs are some of the most inexpensive proteins you can buy! I always purchase them when they go on sale and portion them into two or four pieces in individual bags to freeze. This makes cooking a single portion extremely easy and affordable.

- **Hands-On Time: 5 minutes**
- **Cook Time: 18 minutes**

Serves 1

1 cup water
4 (4-ounce) chicken
   drumsticks
¾ cup sweet chili sauce
1 tablespoon chopped
   green onion

GET CREATIVE!

This method of cooking chicken drumsticks can be used with any sauce! Try barbecue, buffalo, mango habanero, teriyaki, or gochujang sauce. For extra flavor, sprinkle your favorite seasoning blend or rub on the chicken before basting and broiling.

1 Pour water into Instant Pot® and add the trivet. Place drumsticks on trivet.

2 Close the lid; turn the knob to Sealing.

3 Press Manual or Pressure Cook button and adjust time to 10 minutes for fresh chicken legs and 12 minutes for frozen.

4 Preheat oven broiler to high. Line a baking sheet with foil.

5 When the timer beeps, immediately turn the knob from Sealing to Venting, then remove chicken to the prepared baking sheet.

6 Evenly brush chili sauce on chicken, then broil 4 minutes. Flip chicken over and baste on the other side with chili sauce. Broil again 4 minutes until sticky, bubbly, and browned. Remove to a serving plate.

7 Baste with additional sauce and top with green onion. Serve.

PER SERVING

CALORIES: 1,090 | **FAT:** 29g | **PROTEIN:** 88g | **SODIUM:** 3,116mg
FIBER: 0g | **CARBOHYDRATES:** 102g | **SUGAR:** 84g

The Absolute Best Chicken Salad

My favorite restaurant chicken salad sandwich costs almost $10. This delicious sandwich can be made for a fraction of the price! I love making a sandwich with homemade white bread cut into thick slices, but you can also use this to top a green salad, eat it with crackers, or enjoy on a croissant.

- Hands-On Time: 15 minutes
- Cook Time: 20 minutes

Serves 1

1 cup water
1 (8-ounce) boneless, skinless chicken breast
⅛ teaspoon salt
⅛ teaspoon ground black pepper
4½ tablespoons mayonnaise
¼ teaspoon dried dill
⅛ teaspoon garlic powder
¼ teaspoon dried onion flakes
⅛ teaspoon dried basil
⅛ teaspoon seasoned salt
1½ tablespoons finely diced celery
8 grapes, quartered (about ¼ cup)
1 tablespoon cashew halves

EVEN EASIER CHICKEN SALAD

If you're even shorter on time, you can use 1 cup of canned and drained chicken or cut up a rotisserie chicken. Both are excellent options for this recipe and can save even more time!

1 Pour water into Instant Pot® and add chicken. Season chicken with salt and pepper.

2 Close the lid; turn the knob to Sealing.

3 Press Manual or Pressure Cook button and adjust time to 10 minutes.

4 When the timer beeps, allow 10 minutes to naturally release the pressure, then remove the lid.

5 Remove chicken to a small bowl and dice into small pieces. Transfer to the refrigerator while you assemble the rest of the salad.

6 In a separate small bowl, combine mayonnaise, dill, garlic powder, onion flakes, basil, seasoned salt, celery, grapes, and cashews. Add chicken and mix to combine. Transfer to a plate and serve immediately, or refrigerate until ready to eat.

PER SERVING

CALORIES: 750 | FAT: 55g | PROTEIN: 51g | SODIUM: 1,181mg
FIBER: 1g | CARBOHYDRATES: 11g | SUGAR: 7g

Strawberry Barbecue Chicken Salad

Shredded barbecue chicken, juicy strawberries, creamy avocado, bright corn, and savory black beans (and more!) combine to make the prettiest, tastiest salad that would set you back at least $15 at any restaurant. The chicken cooks quickly while you assemble the rest of your salad, and lunch is served!

- **Hands-On Time: 10 minutes**
- **Cook Time: 15 minutes**

Serves 1

1 (8-ounce) boneless, skinless chicken breast

1 cup water

1 teaspoon barbecue dry rub

3 tablespoons barbecue sauce

1½ cups chopped romaine lettuce

2 tablespoons drained and rinsed canned black beans

2 tablespoons sliced strawberries

1¼ tablespoons packaged French fried onions

2 tablespoons sweetened dried cranberries

2 tablespoons corn

1½ tablespoons shredded smoked Gouda cheese

1 tablespoon bacon bits

¼ cup sliced avocado

2 tablespoons ranch dressing

1. To the Instant Pot®, add chicken and water. Season chicken with dry rub.

2. Close the lid; turn the knob to Sealing.

3. Press Manual or Pressure Cook button and adjust time to 10 minutes.

4. When the timer beeps, allow 5 minutes to naturally release the pressure, then remove the lid.

5. Remove chicken to a small bowl and add 1 tablespoon of cooking liquid. Using two forks, shred the chicken.

6. Add barbecue sauce and mix thoroughly. Cool slightly while preparing other ingredients.

7. In a medium bowl, toss together lettuce, beans, strawberries, French fried onions, cranberries, corn, Gouda, bacon bits, and avocado. Top with shredded chicken and ranch dressing to serve.

PER SERVING

CALORIES: 771 | **FAT:** 35g | **PROTEIN:** 60g | **SODIUM:** 1,651mg
FIBER: 11g | **CARBOHYDRATES:** 56g | **SUGAR:** 32g

Cajun Chicken Pasta

Cajun chicken and peppers marry in a creamy sauce that's sure to become a favorite. You can omit the cream, butter, and cheese to make this dish dairy-free, or substitute sausage for the chicken. Feel like shrimp? Stir it in after pressure cooking and cook about 5 minutes or until the shrimp is cooked through. You can also use a different shape pasta or noodle to make this extremely flexible meal.

- **Hands-On Time: 5 minutes**
- **Cook Time: 16 minutes**

Serves 1

1 tablespoon olive oil
1 tablespoon butter
1 cup diced chicken breast
1 teaspoon Cajun seasoning
1 cup chopped bell pepper, any color
½ tablespoon dried onion flakes
¾ cup chicken broth
½ cup heavy cream
1 tablespoon white wine
½ teaspoon minced garlic
½ tablespoon soy sauce
4 ounces uncooked linguine, broken in half
¾ cup diced tomatoes
1 tablespoon shredded Parmesan cheese

CAJUN SEASONING

I recommend starting this dish with 1 teaspoon Cajun seasoning (as written) and then adding more to the finished dish after pressure cooking, if desired, depending on how spicy and salty you like your pasta.

1 On the Instant Pot®, press Sauté button and adjust to High. Add oil and butter. In a small bowl, toss chicken with Cajun seasoning. Add chicken to Instant Pot® and sear chicken 5 minutes, flipping on all sides. Remove chicken and add bell pepper. Sauté 3 minutes and then remove.

2 Add onion flakes, broth, cream, wine, garlic, and soy sauce. Deglaze the pot, scraping all the browned bits off the bottom of the pot.

3 Press Cancel button to turn off the heat. Layer noodles in a crisscross pattern over the liquid to reduce clumping.

4 Pour reserved chicken, its juices, and sautéed pepper over noodles, along with tomatoes. Do not stir.

5 Close the lid; turn the knob to Sealing.

6 Press Manual or Pressure Cook button and adjust time to 8 minutes.

7 When the timer beeps, immediately turn the knob from Sealing to Venting, then remove the lid and stir. If sauce is too thin for your taste, press Sauté button and adjust to High. Stir and reduce sauce 5 minutes or until mostly evaporated. Remove to a serving plate, sprinkle with Parmesan, and serve.

PER SERVING

CALORIES: 1,449 | FAT: 72g | PROTEIN: 75g | SODIUM: 1,620mg
FIBER: 9g | CARBOHYDRATES: 107g | SUGAR: 18g

Chicken Alfredo with Broccoli

There are few recipes that are as classic as Chicken Alfredo with Broccoli. It's total comfort food, and I almost always have all the ingredients needed on hand. My favorite way to utilize this recipe is to make a single portion and split it in half for my two kids. Feel free to use either fresh or frozen broccoli florets in this recipe.

- **Hands-On Time: 5 minutes**
- **Cook Time: 17 minutes**

Serves 1

1 tablespoon butter
¼ cup chicken broth
1 cup heavy cream
½ teaspoon minced garlic
4 ounces uncooked
    fettuccine, broken in half
1 cup diced chicken breast
¼ teaspoon salt
⅛ teaspoon ground
    black pepper
1 cup broccoli florets
¼ cup shredded
    Parmesan cheese

1 To the Instant Pot®, add butter, broth, cream, and garlic. Layer noodles in a crisscross pattern over the liquid to reduce clumping.

2 Add chicken on top of noodles and sprinkle with salt and pepper.

3 Close the lid; turn the knob to Sealing.

4 Press Manual or Pressure Cook button and adjust time to 7 minutes.

5 When the timer beeps, immediately turn the knob from Sealing to Venting, then remove the lid and stir. Immediately add broccoli and replace the lid. Let stand 8–10 minutes until broccoli is completely cooked through. (Alternatively, skip this step and add pre-cooked broccoli.)

6 Add Parmesan, stir, and remove to a serving plate. Serve.

PER SERVING

CALORIES: 1,732 | FAT: 104g | PROTEIN: 81g | SODIUM: 1,379mg
FIBER: 6g | CARBOHYDRATES: 99g | SUGAR: 12g

Chicken with Bacon and Fresh Green Beans

When I buy a small package of chicken breasts, I take them home and chop them into cubes and store in a container in the refrigerator. That way, I can easily throw some chicken into any dish like this one with no added prep.

- **Hands-On Time: 5 minutes**
- **Cook Time: 12 minutes**

Serves 1

1 slice uncooked thick-cut bacon, chopped

⅓ cup diced mushrooms

1 cup diced chicken breast

¼ teaspoon seasoned salt

½ teaspoon Italian seasoning

½ tablespoon dried onion flakes

½ teaspoon minced garlic

¼ cup chicken broth

1 teaspoon soy sauce

5 ounces fresh green beans, trimmed

1. On the Instant Pot®, press Sauté button and adjust to High.

2. Add bacon and sauté about 5 minutes until crispy. Add mushrooms, chicken, salt, Italian seasoning, onion flakes, garlic, broth, and soy sauce. Press Cancel button to turn off the heat and scrape the bottom of the pot with a wooden spoon. Add green beans and stir.

3. Close the lid; turn the knob to Sealing.

4. Press Manual or Pressure Cook button and adjust time to 2 minutes.

5. When the timer beeps, allow 5 minutes to naturally release the pressure, then remove the lid. Transfer to a serving bowl and serve immediately.

PER SERVING

CALORIES: 442 | FAT: 12g | PROTEIN: 63g | SODIUM: 1,019mg FIBER: 4g | CARBOHYDRATES: 14g | SUGAR: 6g

Creamy Tuscan Chicken with Sun-Dried Tomatoes and Kale

This übercreamy and savory dish is delicious over mashed potatoes, rice, buttered noodles, or steamed broccoli.

- **Hands-On Time: 5 minutes**
- **Cook Time: 14 minutes**

Serves 1

1 tablespoon olive oil
1 cup diced chicken breast in 1" cubes
¼ teaspoon Italian seasoning
⅛ teaspoon garlic powder
⅛ teaspoon salt
⅛ teaspoon ground black pepper
½ teaspoon dried onion flakes
½ cup chicken broth
¼ teaspoon soy sauce
1 tablespoon chopped sun-dried tomatoes
½ cup sliced packed kale
¼ cup heavy cream
¼ cup shredded Parmesan cheese

1 On the Instant Pot®, press Sauté button and adjust to High. Add oil.

2 In a small bowl, add chicken. Add Italian seasoning, garlic powder, salt, and pepper. Toss to coat.

3 Add chicken to the hot oil. Sear on each side about 3 minutes until browned. Do not stir while searing. Press Cancel button to turn off the heat.

4 Add onion flakes, broth, soy sauce, and tomatoes. Deglaze the pot, scraping all the browned bits off the bottom of the pot.

5 Close the lid; turn the knob to Sealing.

6 Press Manual or Pressure Cook button and adjust time to 3 minutes.

7 When the timer beeps, immediately turn the knob from Sealing to Venting, then remove the lid. Stir in kale. Replace the lid and let kale wilt down 5 minutes.

8 Remove the lid and stir in cream and Parmesan. Transfer to a serving plate and serve.

PER SERVING

CALORIES: 704 | FAT: 43g | PROTEIN: 62g | SODIUM: 1,300mg
FIBER: 1g | CARBOHYDRATES: 7g | SUGAR: 4g

Bruschetta Chicken

With minimal ingredients, you can transform a boring chicken breast into a delight! Whenever I make bruschetta as an appetizer, I always have leftover tomato mixture. This is a perfect way to use it up!

- **Hands-On Time: 5 minutes**
- **Cook Time: 25 minutes**

Serves 1

Chicken
1 cup water
1 (8-ounce) boneless, skinless chicken breast
⅛ teaspoon salt
⅛ teaspoon ground black pepper
¼ teaspoon Italian seasoning
2 (1-ounce) slices fresh mozzarella cheese

Bruschetta
⅓ cup diced tomatoes
½ tablespoon olive oil
¼ teaspoon balsamic glaze
¼ teaspoon minced garlic
1 teaspoon chopped fresh basil
1/16 teaspoon crushed red pepper flakes
1/16 teaspoon ground black pepper
1/16 teaspoon salt

1 Pour water into Instant Pot® and add the trivet.

2 Place chicken on the trivet, then season with salt, black pepper, and Italian seasoning.

3 Close the lid; turn the knob to Sealing.

4 Press Manual or Pressure Cook button and adjust time to 15 minutes.

5 While the chicken is cooking, prepare Bruschetta. In a small bowl, mix together all Bruschetta ingredients. Let chill in refrigerator until ready to serve.

6 When the timer beeps, allow 5 minutes to naturally release the pressure, then remove the lid. Place mozzarella slices on top of chicken and replace the lid. Let sit 5 minutes with lid on to allow the cheese to melt slightly.

7 Remove to a serving plate and top with Bruschetta. Serve immediately.

PER SERVING

CALORIES: 472 | FAT: 22g | PROTEIN: 60g | SODIUM: 1,020mg
FIBER: 1g | CARBOHYDRATES: 8g | SUGAR: 4g

Chili Cilantro Lime Chicken Thighs and Rice

Here's a one-pot meal with spicy, smoky chicken and rice topped with some fresh lime that brightens up the entire dish and rounds all the flavors out. This recipe uses medium or large bone-in chicken thighs. If your chicken thighs are smaller (about 3–4 ounces), add an additional ½ cup chicken broth or water.

- **Hands-On Time: 5 minutes**
- **Cook Time: 22 minutes**

Serves 1

½ tablespoon olive oil
1 teaspoon dried cilantro
¼ teaspoon chili powder
¼ teaspoon ground cumin
¼ teaspoon salt
¼ teaspoon garlic powder
2 (6–8-ounce) bone-in chicken thighs
½ cup uncooked long-grain white rice
½ cup chicken broth
1 medium lime, quartered

1 On the Instant Pot®, press Sauté button and adjust to High. Add oil and let it heat up until shiny.

2 In a small bowl, combine cilantro, chili powder, cumin, salt, and garlic powder. Season both sides of the chicken with this mixture, about ½ teaspoon per side, reserving any unused seasoning.

3 In the Instant Pot®, add chicken skin-side down and sauté 5 minutes until skin is crispy and golden. Add any remaining seasoning mixture, rice, broth, and ¾ lime.

4 Press Cancel button to turn off the heat and deglaze the pot, scraping all the browned bits off the bottom of the pot.

5 Close the lid; turn the knob to Sealing.

6 Press Manual or Pressure Cook button and adjust time to 12 minutes.

7 When the timer beeps, allow 5 minutes to naturally release the pressure, then remove the lid.

8 Scoop into a serving bowl, then top with the remaining ¼ lime. Serve.

PER SERVING

CALORIES: 1,261 | FAT: 65g | PROTEIN: 71g | SODIUM: 1,378mg
FIBER: 2g | CARBOHYDRATES: 77g | SUGAR: 1g

Chicken Fajitas

The ingredients in these easy Chicken Fajitas cook all together at the same time. Cutting the chicken into bite-sized pieces helps cut the cooking time. Serve this dish with steamed tortillas, sour cream, and any other favorite fajita toppings.

- **Hands-On Time: 7 minutes**
- **Cook Time: 8 minutes**

Serves 1

1 tablespoon olive oil
½ teaspoon chili powder
½ teaspoon salt
½ teaspoon dried oregano
¼ teaspoon garlic powder
¼ teaspoon ground cumin
⅛ teaspoon crushed red
    pepper flakes
1 cup diced chicken breast
    in 1" cubes
2 cups frozen bell pepper mix
⅓ cup water
1 tablespoon soy sauce
1 tablespoon lime juice

1. On the Instant Pot®, press Sauté button and adjust to High. Add oil.

2. In a small bowl, mix together chili powder, salt, oregano, garlic powder, cumin, and red pepper flakes. Remove about half the mixture to a separate small bowl and set aside. Add chicken to one bowl and toss to coat.

3. Add chicken to the hot pot. Sear on each side about 3 minutes until browned. Do not stir while searing. Press Cancel button to turn off the heat.

4. Add bell peppers, water, soy sauce, lime juice, and reserved seasoning mixture. Deglaze the pot, scraping all the browned bits off the bottom of the pot.

5. Close the lid; turn the knob to Sealing.

6. Press Manual or Pressure Cook button and adjust time to 2 minutes.

7. When the timer beeps, immediately turn the knob from Sealing to Venting, then remove the lid.

8. Using tongs, transfer chicken and peppers to a serving plate and serve.

PER SERVING

CALORIES: 476 | FAT: 17g | PROTEIN: 56g | SODIUM: 2,194mg
FIBER: 4g | CARBOHYDRATES: 17g | SUGAR: 8g

Greek Chicken Rice Bowl with Tzatziki Sauce

This homemade Tzatziki Sauce is a great way to use up leftover cucumber, and you can even make it using homemade Instant Pot® yogurt (unsweetened).

- **Hands-On Time: 5 minutes**
- **Cook Time: 15 minutes**

Serves 1

Tzatziki Sauce
4½ tablespoons unsweetened plain Greek-style yogurt
3 tablespoons grated cucumber, liquid squeezed out
1 teaspoon lemon juice
⅛ teaspoon salt
1⁄16 teaspoon ground black pepper
¼ teaspoon dried dill
⅛ teaspoon minced garlic
1 teaspoon olive oil

Chicken Bowl
1 tablespoon olive oil
1 tablespoon butter
Juice and zest of 1 medium lemon
1 cup chicken broth
½ cup uncooked long-grain white rice
1 teaspoon dried oregano
1 teaspoon minced garlic
¼ teaspoon salt
⅛ teaspoon ground black pepper
1 cup chopped chicken breast
1 teaspoon ground lemon pepper

Topping
2 tablespoons diced tomato
2 tablespoons diced red bell pepper
2 tablespoons crumbled feta cheese
2 tablespoons diced red onion
2 tablespoons diced cucumber
2 tablespoons chopped kalamata olives

1. To make the Tzatziki Sauce, in a small bowl or jar, combine all sauce ingredients and refrigerate until ready to eat.

2. To make the Chicken Bowl, to the Instant Pot®, add oil, butter, lemon juice and zest, broth, rice, oregano, garlic, salt, and black pepper. Stir to combine. In a small bowl, toss the chicken in lemon pepper, then spread evenly over rice.

3. Close the lid; turn the knob to Sealing.

4. Press Manual or Pressure Cook button and adjust time to 10 minutes.

5. When the timer beeps, allow 5 minutes to naturally release the pressure, then remove the lid.

6. Scoop the chicken and rice into a serving bowl, then top with tomato, bell pepper, feta, onion, cucumber, and olives. Serve immediately with Tzatziki Sauce.

PER SERVING

CALORIES: 849 | FAT: 44g | PROTEIN: 64g | SODIUM: 2,442mg
FIBER: 2g | CARBOHYDRATES: 40g | SUGAR: 7g

Brown Butter–Garlic Chicken Thighs

Using bone-in chicken thighs gives you unbelievable flavor and juiciness that pairs perfectly with savory brown butter. If you'd prefer to use chicken breast, adjust the cooking time to 15 minutes with a 10-minute natural pressure release.

- **Hands-On Time: 5 minutes**
- **Cook Time: 27 minutes**

Serves 1

2 tablespoons butter
2 (6-ounce) bone-in
   chicken thighs
½ teaspoon garlic powder
½ teaspoon Italian seasoning
½ teaspoon salt
½ teaspoon ground
   black pepper
1 teaspoon minced garlic
½ cup chicken broth

1 On the Instant Pot®, press Sauté button and adjust to High.

2 Add butter and sauté about 5 minutes until browned. Meanwhile, season chicken on both sides with garlic powder, Italian seasoning, salt, and pepper.

3 When butter is browned, add chicken skin-side down and cook 5 minutes without disturbing. Remove chicken to a plate.

4 Add minced garlic and broth. Press Cancel button to turn off the heat and deglaze the pot, scraping all the browned bits off the bottom of the pot. Return chicken to the pot skin-side up.

5 Close the lid; turn the knob to Sealing.

6 Press Manual or Pressure Cook button and adjust time to 12 minutes.

7 When the timer beeps, allow 5 minutes to naturally release the pressure, then remove the lid. Transfer to a serving plate and serve immediately.

PER SERVING

CALORIES: 1,074 | FAT: 79g | PROTEIN: 65g | SODIUM: 1,938mg
FIBER: 0g | CARBOHYDRATES: 4g | SUGAR: 1g

Spicy Pineapple Chicken

Inspired by a popular Chinese restaurant chain, this deliciously sweet and spicy dish is sure to become a "fake-out" (fake takeout) regular! Serve this dish over steamed white or brown rice.

- **Hands-On Time: 7 minutes**
- **Cook Time: 9 minutes**

Serves 1

1 tablespoon olive oil

1 cup diced chicken breast in 1" cubes

1/8 teaspoon garlic powder

1/8 teaspoon salt

1/8 teaspoon ground black pepper

1/16 teaspoon ground ginger

1/8 teaspoon crushed red pepper flakes

3/4 cup diced red bell pepper in 1 1/2" pieces

1/3 cup pineapple chunks

1/4 cup chicken broth

1 tablespoon soy sauce

1/4 cup pineapple juice

1 tablespoon sweet chili sauce

1/2 tablespoon cold water

1/2 tablespoon cornstarch

1 On the Instant Pot®, press Sauté button and adjust to High. Add oil.

2 In a small bowl, season chicken with garlic powder, salt, black pepper, ginger, and red pepper flakes. Toss to coat.

3 Add chicken to the hot oil. Sear on each side about 3 minutes until browned. Do not stir while searing. Press Cancel button to turn off the heat.

4 Add bell pepper, pineapple chunks, broth, soy sauce, pineapple juice, and chili sauce. Deglaze the pot, scraping all the browned bits off the bottom of the pot.

5 Close the lid; turn the knob to Sealing.

6 Press Manual or Pressure Cook button and adjust time to 3 minutes.

7 When the timer beeps, immediately turn the knob from Sealing to Venting, then remove the lid and press Sauté button.

8 In a cup, whisk together the water and cornstarch. Slowly drizzle into the Instant Pot® while stirring. Cook until thickened, about 3 minutes. Transfer to a serving plate and serve.

PER SERVING

CALORIES: 544 | **FAT:** 17g | **PROTEIN:** 58g | **SODIUM:** 4,372mg
FIBER: 4g | **CARBOHYDRATES:** 31g | **SUGAR:** 20g

Honey-Sesame Chicken and Broccoli

I love all the flavors of this sweet and spicy dish with sticky honey-sesame sauce! If you prefer, you can swap the broccoli for another vegetable such as fresh green beans or baby bok choy.

- **Hands-On Time: 2 minutes**
- **Cook Time: 10 minutes**

Serves 1

¼ cup water

2 tablespoons honey

1½ tablespoons brown sugar

1 tablespoon soy sauce

1 tablespoon ketchup

½ tablespoon sriracha sauce

½ tablespoon sesame oil

½ teaspoon minced garlic

1 cup diced chicken breast in 1" pieces

1½ cups broccoli florets

½ teaspoon sesame seeds

1 cup cooked white rice

1   In a small bowl, whisk together water, honey, brown sugar, soy sauce, ketchup, sriracha, oil, and garlic.

2   Add chicken to the Instant Pot® and pour sauce over it.

3   Close the lid; turn the knob to Sealing.

4   Press Manual or Pressure Cook button and adjust time to 2 minutes.

5   When the timer beeps, immediately turn the knob from Sealing to Venting, then remove the lid. Press Sauté button and adjust to High.

6   Add broccoli to chicken and mix into sauce. Sauté 6–8 minutes until broccoli is cooked through and sauce is reduced to a thick and sticky consistency.

7   Sprinkle with sesame seeds. Serve over rice.

PER SERVING

CALORIES: 830 | **FAT:** 12g | **PROTEIN:** 61g | **SODIUM:** 1,336mg
FIBER: 5g | **CARBOHYDRATES:** 116g | **SUGAR:** 62g

Fish and Seafood

I used to be intimidated by the thought of cooking fish and seafood in my Instant Pot®, but now I swear by it! These proteins from the sea cook in mere minutes (I'm talking 0–2 minutes for most!), and the method is nearly foolproof.

Perhaps the greatest advantage to cooking seafood for one is the cost. Purchasing seafood for a larger group often becomes prohibitive because it is usually more expensive than poultry, beef, or pork. Most grocery stores have a seafood counter where you can purchase exactly what and how much you need, such as a cluster of crab legs or a single lobster tail. You can easily place a frozen piece of fish in the Instant Pot® and cook it in minutes, and it is often a much fresher, healthier dish than your usual choice.

Try the delectable New England Clam Chowder (it conveniently uses a single can of clams), Lemony Shrimp Scampi, or Brown Butter Angel Hair Pasta with Scallops and Tomatoes. Also, the Quick and Easy Shrimp Boil is fun to make and costs a fraction of what the restaurants charge. These affordable and delicious meals will have you hooked!

New England Clam Chowder

Smoky bacon, chewy clams, and chunks of potato that simply melt in your mouth will make you want to make two portions! This recipe uses a single 3-ounce can of chopped clams, so there's no waste. Make sure you use thick-cut bacon, or there won't be adequate fat left in the pan to sauté the vegetables. If you have to use regular-cut bacon, add ½ tablespoon butter to the pot after scooping out the bacon.

- **Hands-On Time: 5 minutes**
- **Cook Time: 9 minutes**

Serves 1

1 slice uncooked thick-cut bacon, chopped

¾ cup diced red potatoes

1½ tablespoons diced yellow onion

¼ cup diced celery

½ teaspoon salt

⅛ teaspoon ground black pepper

⅛ teaspoon dried thyme

½ cup chicken broth

1 (3-ounce) can chopped clams in clam juice, drained but juice reserved

1 tablespoon white wine

1 bay leaf

2 tablespoons all-purpose flour

1 cup heavy cream

1 teaspoon chopped parsley

1 On the Instant Pot®, press Sauté button and adjust to High. Add bacon and sauté about 5 minutes until crispy. Using a slotted spoon, remove bacon and set aside, leaving the bacon grease in the pot.

2 Add potatoes, onion, celery, salt, pepper, and thyme. Sauté 1 minute, then add broth, reserved clam juice, and wine. Deglaze the pot, scraping all the browned bits off the bottom of the pot. Add bay leaf. Press Cancel button to turn off the heat.

3 Close the lid; turn the knob to Sealing.

4 Press Manual or Pressure Cook button and adjust time to 3 minutes.

5 When the timer beeps, immediately turn the knob from Sealing to Venting, then remove the lid. Press Sauté button and adjust to High.

6 In a small bowl, whisk flour into cream until completely combined. Pour into pot. Bring chowder up to a boil, then press Cancel button. Remove bay leaf and stir in clams. Ladle into a bowl and serve topped with parsley and bacon.

PER SERVING

CALORIES: 1,313 | FAT: 106g | PROTEIN: 34g | SODIUM: 2,232mg
FIBER: 3g | CARBOHYDRATES: 44g | SUGAR: 10g

Spicy Clam Pasta

Because this pasta doesn't have a heavy sauce, it's a perfect light yet satisfying quick meal to make on busy afternoons or as lunches for one. I like to make this pasta ahead of time if I need to take lunch out of the house because it reheats very well, and it tastes delicious at room temperature or even chilled. Don't skip the crushed red pepper, as it gives the dish that slight heat.

- **Hands-On Time: 5 minutes**
- **Cook Time: 12 minutes**

Serves 1

1 (3-ounce) can chopped clams in clam juice, drained but juice reserved
¼ cup chicken broth
¼ cup lemon juice
⅛ teaspoon crushed red pepper flakes
1 teaspoon dried onion flakes
2 tablespoons butter
¼ teaspoon lemon zest
¼ teaspoon salt
¼ teaspoon minced garlic
4 ounces uncooked spaghetti, broken in half

1 To the Instant Pot®, add reserved clam juice, broth, lemon juice, red pepper flakes, onion flakes, butter, lemon zest, salt, and garlic. Stir to combine. Layer spaghetti in a crisscross pattern over the liquid to reduce clumping.

2 Close the lid; turn the knob to Sealing.

3 Press Manual or Pressure Cook button and adjust time to 7 minutes.

4 When the timer beeps, immediately turn the knob from Sealing to Venting, then remove the lid. Press Sauté button and adjust to High. Stir and reduce sauce 5 minutes until mostly evaporated. When ready to serve, add clams and ladle into a bowl. Serve.

PER SERVING

CALORIES: 744 | FAT: 23g | PROTEIN: 33g | SODIUM: 929mg
FIBER: 4g | CARBOHYDRATES: 95g | SUGAR: 5g

Quick and Easy Shrimp Boil

You can make this incredibly beautiful shrimp boil in the Instant Pot® in a couple of minutes and for a fraction of the price at a restaurant. If you want to add additional seafood such as crab, add it to the Instant Pot® at the same time as the shrimp. The cook time will stay the same.

- **Hands-On Time: 5 minutes**
- **Cook Time: 11 minutes**

Serves 1

1 cup chicken broth

1 teaspoon minced garlic

2 medium red potatoes, quartered

1 medium ear corn, husked

1 (3-ounce) link andouille sausage, cut into 4 pieces on the bias

½ tablespoon Old Bay seasoning

1 cup peeled and deveined extra-large shrimp

3 tablespoons butter, melted

½ medium lemon, for serving

1 tablespoon chopped fresh parsley

FRESH OR FROZEN SHRIMP?

For convenience, I use frozen shrimp that has already been shelled and cleaned for me. However, you may use fresh shrimp and cook for the same amount of time.

1 To the Instant Pot®, add broth and garlic. Add the trivet.

2 Add potatoes, corn, and sausage, then sprinkle Old Bay seasoning over everything.

3 Close the lid; turn the knob to Sealing.

4 Press Manual or Pressure Cook button and adjust time to 3 minutes.

5 When the timer beeps, immediately turn the knob from Sealing to Venting, then remove the lid.

6 Add shrimp, stir, then immediately replace the lid and wait 5–8 minutes until the shrimp is pink and cooked through.

7 To serve, remove everything to a large bowl and serve with a side of butter, lemon, and sprinkle of parsley.

PER SERVING

CALORIES: 1,033 | FAT: 49g | PROTEIN: 57g | SODIUM: 3,663mg
FIBER: 11g | CARBOHYDRATES: 93g | SUGAR: 13g

Garlic-Chili Fish Tacos with Spicy Lime Crema

I like using tilapia for fish tacos for its light texture and taste. It's also incredibly affordable and readily available. Using individually packaged frozen fish fillets is the most economical way to cook fish for one—just take out a piece for any recipe, and you'll always have fresh fish.

- Hands-On Time: 15 minutes
- Cook Time: 2 minutes

Serves 1

Fish
½ tablespoon olive oil
½ teaspoon minced garlic
⅛ teaspoon smoked paprika
⅛ teaspoon chili powder
⅛ teaspoon ground cumin
¼ teaspoon salt
⅛ teaspoon Cajun seasoning
2 (4.5-ounce) frozen tilapia fillets
1 cup water

Spicy Lime Crema
2 tablespoons sour cream
1 tablespoon mayonnaise
1 teaspoon lime juice
⅛ teaspoon garlic salt
⅛ teaspoon salt
½ teaspoon sriracha sauce

For Serving
3 small tortillas, warmed
⅓ cup shredded cabbage
1½ tablespoons pico de gallo
1 tablespoon chopped cilantro
½ medium lime

1 To make the Fish, in a small bowl, mix together oil and all the spices, then spread evenly over both sides of fillets.

2 Pour water into Instant Pot® and add the trivet. Place fish on trivet.

3 Close the lid; turn the knob to Sealing.

4 Press Manual or Pressure Cook button and adjust time to 2 minutes.

5 When the timer beeps, immediately turn the knob from Sealing to Venting, then remove the lid and carefully transfer fish to a small bowl.

6 In a separate small bowl, combine all Spicy Lime Crema ingredients and refrigerate until ready to use.

7 To serve, transfer tortillas to a serving plate. Evenly break up the fish between tortillas. Top with cabbage, pico de gallo, Spicy Lime Crema, cilantro, and a squeeze of lime.

PER SERVING

CALORIES: 700 | FAT: 29g | PROTEIN: 55g | SODIUM: 2,095mg
FIBER: 3g | CARBOHYDRATES: 51g | SUGAR: 6g

Creamy Pesto Tilapia with Sun-Dried Tomatoes and Artichokes

If you love pesto, you'll love this creamy dish of tilapia with tomatoes and artichokes. This dish would be equally delicious using any white fish such as cod or halibut. Serve over your favorite carb—noodles, rice pilaf, mashed potatoes—or even steamed broccoli.

- **Hands-On Time: 5 minutes**
- **Cook Time: 2 minutes**

Serves 1

1 tablespoon butter

3 tablespoons chopped sun-dried tomatoes

½ cup artichoke heart quarters

1 teaspoon lemon juice

⅛ teaspoon salt

⅛ teaspoon ground black pepper

½ cup chicken broth

1 tablespoon basil pesto

2 (4.5-ounce) frozen tilapia fillets

2 tablespoons heavy cream

3 tablespoons shredded Parmesan cheese

1 To the Instant Pot® add butter, tomatoes, artichokes, lemon juice, salt, pepper, and broth.

2 Spread pesto all over the tops of fillets and place on trivet. Lower the trivet into the Instant Pot®.

3 Close the lid; turn the knob to Sealing.

4 Press Manual or Pressure Cook button and adjust time to 2 minutes.

5 When the timer beeps, immediately turn the knob from Sealing to Venting, then remove the lid and carefully transfer fish to a serving plate.

6 Stir cream and Parmesan into the sauce. Ladle sauce over fish and serve.

PER SERVING

CALORIES: 626 | FAT: 35g | PROTEIN: 58g | SODIUM: 1,352mg
FIBER: 9g | CARBOHYDRATES: 19g | SUGAR: 7g

Lemony Shrimp Scampi

You won't be able to believe how incredibly delicious this shrimp scampi sauce is! The beauty of making this single generous portion is that you can enjoy it in a variety of ways—toss it with your favorite cooked pasta, spoon it over rice or mashed potatoes, or dip a small loaf of crusty sourdough bread into it.

- **Hands-On Time: 2 minutes**
- **Cook Time: 0 minutes**

Serves 1

¼ cup butter

1 tablespoon dried onion flakes

1 teaspoon minced garlic

3 tablespoons white wine

3 tablespoons chicken broth

3 tablespoons lemon juice

½ teaspoon salt

⅛ teaspoon ground
    black pepper

½ teaspoon chopped parsley

⅛ teaspoon crushed
    red pepper flakes

2 cups peeled and deveined
    extra-large shrimp

2 tablespoons heavy cream

1 To the Instant Pot®, add all ingredients and stir.

2 Close the lid; turn the knob to Sealing.

3 Press Manual or Pressure Cook button and adjust time to 0 minutes.

4 When the timer beeps, immediately turn the knob from Sealing to Venting, then remove the lid and stir about 1 minute until shrimp is completely cooked and pink. Transfer to a bowl and serve.

PER SERVING

CALORIES: 882 | FAT: 57g | PROTEIN: 64g | SODIUM: 3,921mg
FIBER: 1g | CARBOHYDRATES: 14g | SUGAR: 4g

Addictive Shrimp Alfredo

Now you can enjoy one of the best Alfredos I've ever had in a perfect single portion! Make sure you scatter the noodles as best as you can to prevent sticking.

- **Hands-On Time: 5 minutes**
- **Cook Time: 13 minutes**

Serves 1

¾ cup chicken broth

1 cup heavy cream

½ teaspoon minced garlic

½ teaspoon salt

⅛ teaspoon ground black pepper

½ teaspoon chopped parsley

1 tablespoon butter

4 ounces uncooked fettuccine, broken in half

2 cups peeled and deveined extra-large shrimp

¾ cup shredded Parmesan cheese

1 To the Instant Pot®, add broth, cream, garlic, salt, pepper, parsley, and butter; stir. Layer fettuccine in a crisscross pattern over the liquid to reduce clumping. Pat noodles down to submerge them as much as possible.

2 Close the lid; turn the knob to Sealing.

3 Press Manual or Pressure Cook button and adjust time to 7 minutes.

4 When the timer beeps, immediately turn the knob from Sealing to Venting, then remove the lid. Add shrimp and stir 6 minutes until shrimp is completely cooked through and pasta has thickened.

5 Add Parmesan, stir completely, then transfer to a bowl and serve.

PER SERVING

CALORIES: 1,765 | FAT: 113g | PROTEIN: 75g | SODIUM: 4,251mg
FIBER: 4g | CARBOHYDRATES: 97g | SUGAR: 11g

Edamame, Shrimp, and Quinoa Salad

I love all the flavors, colors, and textures of this healthy salad. It's easy to make for a full lunch, or to serve as a side dish for multiple meals. Feel free to add your favorite fresh vegetables.

- **Hands-On Time: 10 minutes**
- **Cook Time: 12 minutes**

Serves 1

½ cup uncooked quinoa, rinsed

1 cup water

½ cup frozen peeled and deveined extra-small shrimp

½ cup shelled edamame

1 tablespoon lemon juice

1 tablespoon lime juice

2 tablespoons olive oil

½ tablespoon rice wine vinegar

1 tablespoon chopped cilantro

¼ teaspoon salt

¹⁄₁₆ teaspoon ground black pepper

¼ cup cherry tomatoes

¼ cup diced cucumber

1 To the Instant Pot®, add quinoa and water.

2 Close the lid; turn the knob to Sealing.

3 Press Manual or Pressure Cook button and adjust time to 2 minutes.

4 When the timer beeps, allow 10 minutes to naturally release the pressure, then remove the lid and stir in shrimp and edamame. Take the Instant Pot® liner out of the base and let stand 8 minutes to cool the quinoa and warm the shrimp and edamame.

5 In a small bowl, whisk together lemon juice, lime juice, oil, vinegar, cilantro, salt, and pepper.

6 Add tomatoes and cucumber to the quinoa mixture, then add dressing and toss. Transfer to a bowl and serve immediately, or refrigerate 2–4 hours and serve chilled.

PER SERVING

CALORIES: 746 | FAT: 35g | PROTEIN: 38g | SODIUM: 1,242mg
FIBER: 13g | CARBOHYDRATES: 68g | SUGAR: 3g

Traditional Japanese Udon

Udon ("OO-don") noodles are a staple in my house and in Japanese cooking. This one-pot method cooks the broth and the noodles at the same time in minutes—it's become my go-to lunch, and I don't think I'll be able to make this dish on the stove ever again! Udon noodles always come frozen in individually sized portions, so this is the perfect dish to throw together for one!

- **Hands-On Time: 2 minutes**
- **Cook Time: 1 minute**

Serves 1

1 (250-gram) block frozen udon noodles

1½ cups water

2 teaspoons dashi powder

¼ teaspoon salt

1 teaspoon sugar

1 tablespoon soy sauce

¼ cup dried shiitake mushrooms

1 tablespoon mirin

1 tablespoon minced green onion

1⁄16 teaspoon shichimi togarashi

1 To the Instant Pot®, add noodles, water, dashi powder, salt, sugar, soy sauce, mushrooms, and mirin.

2 Close the lid; turn the knob to Sealing.

3 Press Manual or Pressure Cook button and adjust time to 1 minute.

4 When the timer beeps, immediately turn the knob from Sealing to Venting, then remove the lid.

5 Pour the contents into a serving bowl, top with green onion and togarashi, and serve immediately.

PER SERVING

CALORIES: 386 | **FAT:** 1g | **PROTEIN:** 11g | **SODIUM:** 3,029mg **FIBER:** 1g | **CARBOHYDRATES:** 84g | **SUGAR:** 12g

JAPANESE INGREDIENTS

Shichimi togarashi is a Japanese blend of seven spices that includes chili peppers and black sesame seeds. Make sure you don't accidentally purchase ichimi togarashi, which means "one spice." (*Shichi* means "seven"; *ichi* means "one.") Mirin is a Japanese rice wine that is the secret to most Japanese cooking. It is a sweet and savory ingredient that adds that extra specialness to a dish. If you don't have mirin, you can omit it or substitute sugar water.

Spicy Honey-Garlic Salmon

You'll love this sweet, savory, and spicy dish that's perfect for a single serving.

- **Hands-On Time: 2 minutes**
- **Cook Time: 11 minutes**

Serves 1

¼ cup soy sauce

2 tablespoons honey

½ tablespoon apple cider
  vinegar

½ tablespoon olive oil

1½ tablespoons brown sugar

½ teaspoon minced garlic

1 (5-ounce) frozen salmon fillet

1 In the Instant Pot®, stir all ingredients together.

2 Close the lid; turn the knob to Sealing.

3 Press Manual or Pressure Cook button and adjust time to 3 minutes.

4 When the timer beeps, immediately turn the knob from Sealing to Venting, then remove the lid and transfer fish to a plate or bowl.

5 On the Instant Pot®, press Sauté button and adjust to High. Cook sauce about 8 minutes until reduced and thickened.

6 Spoon 1 tablespoon sauce over fish and serve.

PER SERVING

CALORIES: 501 | FAT: 15g | PROTEIN: 34g | SODIUM: 3,569mg
FIBER: 1g | CARBOHYDRATES: 59g | SUGAR: 55g

Instant Pot® Crab Legs (pictured)

Skip the Chinese buffet or expensive steak house and enjoy a vat of deliciously succulent, easy crab legs at home!

- **Hands-On Time: 2 minutes**
- **Cook Time: 1 minute**

Serves 1

1 cup water

1 pound crab legs

⅛ teaspoon Old Bay seasoning

2 tablespoons clarified butter

½ medium lemon,
  cut into wedges

1 Pour water into Instant Pot® and add the trivet.

2 Add crab legs and sprinkle with Old Bay seasoning.

3 Close the lid; turn the knob to Sealing.

4 Press Manual or Pressure Cook button and adjust time to 1 minute, then press Pressure button and adjust to Low Pressure.

5 When the timer beeps, immediately turn the knob from Sealing to Venting, then remove the lid immediately. Overcooked crab is very flaky and not tender, so it must be removed from the heat source as soon as possible.

6 Remove crab to a plate and serve with butter and lemon.

PER SERVING

CALORIES: 488 | FAT: 22g | PROTEIN: 62g | SODIUM: 2,847mg
FIBER: 0g | CARBOHYDRATES: 0g | SUGAR: 0g

Instant Pot® Lobster Tails

Treat yourself with some gorgeous, perfectly cooked lobster tails! Lobsters can be purchased individually from your local butcher, which is perfect for single-serve cooking because it's much more affordable.

- **Hands-On Time: 10 minutes**
- **Cook Time: 0 minutes**

Serves 1

2 (6-ounce) lobster tails
⅛ teaspoon Old Bay seasoning
1 cup water
½ teaspoon minced garlic
½ teaspoon salt
½ teaspoon chopped parsley
2 tablespoons clarified butter
2 lemon wedges

1 Using kitchen shears, cut down the center of each lobster tail all the way to the base of the tail. Carefully crack open the lobster to expose the meat underneath, then slide your finger on the underside of the meat to loosen it from the bottom of the shell. Pop the meat up and above the shell so it lies gently on the outer shell but is still connected to the tail. Sprinkle the lobster tails with Old Bay seasoning, then set aside.

2 To the Instant Pot®, add water, garlic, and salt. Add the trivet.

3 Place lobsters on trivet.

4 Close the lid; turn the knob to Sealing.

5 Press Manual or Pressure Cook button and adjust time to 0 minutes, then press Pressure button and adjust to Low Pressure.

6 When the timer beeps, immediately turn the knob from Sealing to Venting, then remove the lid. Take the internal temperature of lobster. It should be 140°F. If it is a little under, replace the lid and wait 2 minutes before checking again. Lobster is extremely delicate and easy to overcook.

7 Remove lobster tails to a plate and top with parsley. Serve with butter and lemon.

PER SERVING

CALORIES: 354 | **FAT:** 23g | **PROTEIN:** 33g | **SODIUM:** 899mg
FIBER: 0g | **CARBOHYDRATES:** 0g | **SUGAR:** 0g

Cheesy Cajun Shrimp and Grits

Spicy, creamy, acidic, smoky, and savory—this dish is the perfect blend of flavors to enjoy in the Instant Pot® in minutes!

- Hands-On Time: 5 minutes
- Cook Time: 16 minutes

Serves 1

¼ cup grits

½ cup whole milk

1 cup chicken broth, divided

¹⁄₁₆ teaspoon salt

2 tablespoons butter, divided

2 tablespoons minced yellow onion

1 teaspoon minced garlic

½ cup diced tomatoes

¾ cup diced andouille sausage (about 1 sausage)

¼ teaspoon Cajun seasoning

3 tablespoons shredded Cheddar cheese

1 cup peeled and deveined extra-large shrimp

½ tablespoon chopped fresh parsley

1 To a 6" cake pan, add grits, milk, ½ cup broth, and salt. Set aside.

2 On the Instant Pot®, press Sauté button and adjust to High. Add 1 tablespoon butter. Add onion and garlic and sauté 1 minute. Add tomatoes, sausage, Cajun seasoning, and remaining ½ cup broth. Press Cancel button to turn off the heat and add the trivet on top of mixture.

3 Place cake pan on trivet. Close the lid; turn the knob to Sealing.

4 Press Manual or Pressure Cook button and adjust time to 10 minutes.

5 When the timer beeps, immediately turn the knob from Sealing to Venting, then remove the lid and carefully remove the cake pan. Stir remaining 1 tablespoon butter and Cheddar into grits. Cover and set aside.

6 On the Instant Pot®, press Sauté button, then stir in shrimp. Sauté shrimp about 5 minutes until fully cooked.

7 Spoon grits onto a plate, then top with shrimp mixture. Garnish with parsley and serve immediately.

PER SERVING

CALORIES: 886 | FAT: 48g | PROTEIN: 59g | SODIUM: 3,590mg
FIBER: 5g | CARBOHYDRATES: 47g | SUGAR: 10g

Simple Lemon Salmon with Zesty Dill Sauce

This is a very healthy steamed salmon fillet that cooks with dill and lemon, which infuses the salmon with citrus and earthy tones. You'll love the simple yet delicious sauce to pair it with. I like serving this fillet with steamed broccoli, green beans, or rice.

- **Hands-On Time: 5 minutes**
- **Cook Time: 5 minutes**

Serves 1

Salmon

¼ cup water

¼ cup lemon juice

2 sprigs fresh dill

1 (8-ounce) skinless salmon fillet

¼ teaspoon kosher salt

¼ teaspoon ground black pepper

3 slices lemon

Zesty Dill Sauce

1½ tablespoons sour cream

1½ tablespoons mayonnaise

½ teaspoon minced fresh dill

¼ teaspoon Dijon mustard

¼ teaspoon lemon zest

½ tablespoon lemon juice

⅛ teaspoon garlic salt

1 To the Instant Pot®, add water, lemon juice, and fresh dill. Add the trivet.

2 Sprinkle salmon with salt and pepper on all sides, then place lemon slices on top of salmon. Place salmon on the trivet.

3 Close the lid; turn the knob to Sealing.

4 Press Manual or Pressure Cook button and adjust time to 5 minutes.

5 While the fish cooks, prepare the Zesty Dill Sauce. In a small bowl, combine all sauce ingredients and refrigerate until ready to use.

6 When the timer beeps, immediately turn the knob from Sealing to Venting, then remove the lid.

7 Transfer salmon to a plate and serve immediately with dill sauce.

PER SERVING

CALORIES: 500 | FAT: 31g | PROTEIN: 46g | SODIUM: 1,095mg FIBER: 0g | CARBOHYDRATES: 2g | SUGAR: 1g

Salmon and Crispy Baby Potatoes with Feta-Dill Sauce

This one-pot meal cooks the salmon and potatoes at the same time, making this a perfect dish to make for yourself for lunch or dinner.

- **Hands-On Time: 7 minutes**
- **Cook Time: 13 minutes**

Serves 1

Salmon and Potatoes

1 cup water

¼ teaspoon minced garlic

½ teaspoon salt

1 cup halved baby potatoes

1 (8-ounce) salmon fillet

¼ teaspoon kosher salt

¼ teaspoon ground black pepper

½ teaspoon Old Bay seasoning

1 tablespoon butter

½ tablespoon minced fresh parsley

Feta-Dill Sauce

1 tablespoon sour cream

2 tablespoons mayonnaise

1 tablespoon crumbled feta cheese

½ tablespoon lemon juice

⅛ teaspoon salt

1 To the Instant Pot®, add water, garlic, salt, and potatoes. Add the trivet.

2 Sprinkle salmon with kosher salt and pepper on all sides. Place salmon on the trivet.

3 Close the lid; turn the knob to Sealing.

4 Press Manual or Pressure Cook button and adjust time to 5 minutes.

5 While the fish cooks, prepare sauce. In a small bowl, combine all Feta-Dill Sauce ingredients and refrigerate until ready to use.

6 When the timer beeps, immediately turn the knob from Sealing to Venting, then remove the lid. Transfer salmon to a plate and cover.

7 Drain potatoes into a small bowl and toss with Old Bay seasoning. On the Instant Pot®, press Sauté button and adjust to High.

8 When the Instant Pot® display reads "HOT," add butter and potatoes. Lay potatoes in the pot cut-side down. Do not flip or move the potatoes. Cook about 5–8 minutes until extremely crispy. Transfer to a serving plate, sprinkle with parsley, and serve immediately with salmon and Feta-Dill Sauce.

PER SERVING

CALORIES: 794 | FAT: 48g | PROTEIN: 50g | SODIUM: 1,601mg
FIBER: 3g | CARBOHYDRATES: 33g | SUGAR: 2g

Brown Butter Angel Hair Pasta with Scallops and Tomatoes

This is one of the prettiest, most delicious recipes in this chapter. Instead of using large scallops, which are both easy to overcook and more expensive, use frozen bay scallops that are perfectly sized, tender, and much more affordable.

- Hands-On Time: 3 minutes
- Cook Time: 6 minutes

Serves 1

1 cup chicken broth
1 teaspoon minced garlic
⅛ teaspoon crushed
   red pepper flakes
3½ ounces uncooked angel
   hair pasta, broken in half
½ cup frozen bay scallops
2 tablespoons brown butter
⅓ cup halved cherry tomatoes
2 tablespoons heavy cream
1 tablespoon minced
   fresh parsley

1 To the Instant Pot®, add broth, garlic, and red pepper flakes. Layer pasta in a crisscross pattern over the liquid to reduce clumping.

2 Close the lid; turn the knob to Sealing.

3 Press Manual or Pressure Cook button and adjust time to 1 minute.

4 When the timer beeps, immediately turn the knob from Sealing to Venting, then remove the lid.

5 Immediately stir in scallops, brown butter, tomatoes, and cream. Stir 5 minutes until scallops are completely cooked through.

6 Transfer to a serving dish and top with parsley. Serve.

PER SERVING

CALORIES: 816 | FAT: 40g | PROTEIN: 30g | SODIUM: 1,387mg
FIBER: 4g | CARBOHYDRATES: 83g | SUGAR: 6g

Creamy Scallop Risotto with Spinach and Lemon

Creamy and delicious risotto is mixed with spinach and topped with baby scallops. Then it's all tossed in brown butter to give you an entire meal that's glamorous but incredibly easy!

- **Hands-On Time: 5 minutes**
- **Cook Time: 34 minutes**

Serves 1

½ cup frozen bay scallops
⅛ teaspoon salt
⅛ teaspoon ground black pepper
2 tablespoons butter, divided
½ tablespoon dried onion flakes
½ teaspoon minced garlic
½ cup uncooked Arborio rice
1 cup chicken broth
1 tablespoon white wine
1½ tablespoons lemon juice
½ cup packed spinach

USING SEA SCALLOPS

You may make this using full-sized (sea) scallops, but do not stir them in as directed. Instead, wash and clean the scallops, then pat completely dry and season with salt and pepper. Heat 1 tablespoon olive oil and 1 tablespoon butter in a pan and sauté scallops on each side about 2–3 minutes, being careful not to overcook them. Place cooked scallops on top of finished risotto.

1 On the Instant Pot®, press Sauté button and adjust to High.

2 Season scallops with salt and pepper. Add 1 tablespoon butter to the pot and swirl about 3 minutes until browned. Add scallops and stir about 3–5 minutes until fully cooked. Remove to a serving plate.

3 Add remaining 1 tablespoon butter, onion flakes, garlic, and rice. Stir 2–3 minutes to toast the rice. Add broth, wine, and lemon juice and deglaze the pot, scraping all the browned bits off the bottom of the pot. Press Cancel button to turn off the heat.

4 Close the lid; turn the knob to Sealing.

5 Press Manual or Pressure Cook button and adjust time to 10 minutes.

6 When the timer beeps, allow 10 minutes to naturally release the pressure, then remove the lid.

7 Stir spinach into risotto about 3 minutes until wilted. Stir in scallops and brown butter right before serving. Transfer to a serving plate and serve immediately.

PER SERVING

CALORIES: 680 | **FAT:** 22g | **PROTEIN:** 23g | **SODIUM:** 1,684mg
FIBER: 4g | **CARBOHYDRATES:** 89g | **SUGAR:** 3g

9

Vegetarian Main Dishes

These vegetarian dishes are so flavorful and substantial on their own that you won't ever miss the meat! I have a goal to incorporate more vegetables into my diet—and even eat a completely vegetarian diet for limited time periods—and these recipes helped me discover new and creative ways to make delicious meals for myself and my family.

These recipes do not contain meat but can easily be adapted to include meat or meat products like chicken broth if you prefer. Adding alternative proteins can bulk up any of these dishes.

In this chapter, you'll find traditional favorites like Creamy Fettuccine Alfredo and Easy Mac 'n' Cheese, as well as some new dishes like Spaghetti Squash with Lemon-Cream Sauce, or (our favorite) Angel Hair Margherita Pasta. Whether you eat meat on a regular basis or not, I'm confident you'll love the flavorful and hearty meals in this chapter as much as any other dish—without having to designate it as "vegetarian"!

Creamy Fettuccine Alfredo

I find that fettuccine Alfredo never reheats very well, so I prefer to make it fresh every time. Making it in a single portion is the best solution to perfectly creamy, never-separated fettuccine Alfredo. Try adding a tablespoon of pesto sauce to your Alfredo for a yummy variation.

- **Hands-On Time: 5 minutes**
- **Cook Time: 12 minutes**

Serves 1

¾ cup vegetable broth

1 cup heavy cream

½ teaspoon minced garlic

¾ teaspoon salt

⅛ teaspoon ground black pepper

½ teaspoon dried parsley

1 tablespoon butter

4 ounces uncooked fettuccine, broken in half

¾ cup vegetarian shredded Parmesan cheese

1 To the Instant Pot®, add broth, cream, garlic, salt, pepper, parsley, and butter. Stir. Layer fettuccine in a crisscross pattern over the liquid to reduce clumping. Pat noodles down to submerge them as much as possible.

2 Close the lid; turn the knob to Sealing.

3 Press Manual or Pressure Cook button and adjust time to 7 minutes.

4 When the timer beeps, immediately turn the knob from Sealing to Venting, then remove the lid.

5 Stir, then slowly add Parmesan while stirring. Cook about 5 minutes until thickened. Transfer to a bowl and serve.

PER SERVING

CALORIES: 1,600 | **FAT:** 111g | **PROTEIN:** 43g | **SODIUM:** 3,459mg
FIBER: 4g | **CARBOHYDRATES:** 96g | **SUGAR:** 12g

Vegetable-Stuffed Peppers

Stuffed to the brim with vegetables, cheese, and sauce, this incredibly hearty pepper with tomato sauce will become a weekly staple in your home.

- **Hands-On Time: 8 minutes**
- **Cook Time: 15 minutes**

Serves 1

¼ cup diced portobello mushroom

¼ cup cooked brown rice

¼ cup diced tomatoes

2 tablespoons drained and rinsed canned black beans

½ teaspoon dried onion flakes

½ teaspoon soy sauce

½ teaspoon minced garlic

¼ teaspoon Italian seasoning

4 tablespoons tomato sauce, divided

4 tablespoons shredded Cheddar cheese, divided

¼ teaspoon salt

1 large green bell pepper, top removed, seeded, and cored

1 cup water

1 In a small bowl, combine mushroom, rice, tomatoes, beans, onion flakes, soy sauce, garlic, Italian seasoning, 1 tablespoon tomato sauce, 2 tablespoons Cheddar, and salt. Scoop the mixture into hollowed-out bell pepper.

2 Top filling with 1 tablespoon tomato sauce and remaining 2 tablespoons Cheddar.

3 Pour water into Instant Pot® and add the trivet. Place bell pepper on trivet.

4 Close the lid; turn the knob to Sealing.

5 Press Manual or Pressure Cook button and adjust time to 15 minutes.

6 When the timer beeps, immediately turn the knob from Sealing to Venting, then remove the lid.

7 Using tongs, carefully remove the pepper to a plate and spread remaining 2 tablespoons tomato sauce on top. Let stand 5 minutes, then serve.

PER SERVING

CALORIES: 250 | FAT: 0g | PROTEIN: 13g | SODIUM: 1,225mg
FIBER: 8g | CARBOHYDRATES: 31g | SUGAR: 8g

Pasta Primavera

This easy and healthy Pasta Primavera uses a variety of fresh vegetables and delicious cheese tortellini in a light sauce. Use your favorite vegetables or even a frozen vegetable mix to make it even easier!

- **Hands-On Time: 2 minutes**
- **Cook Time: 9 minutes**

Serves 1

1 cup uncooked cheese tortellini
½ cup vegetable broth
½ cup sliced zucchini
½ cup sliced mushrooms
½ cup diced tomatoes
¼ teaspoon Italian seasoning
½ teaspoon minced garlic
⅛ teaspoon salt
½ cup packed spinach
3 tablespoons heavy cream
3 tablespoons vegetarian shredded Parmesan cheese

1 To the Instant Pot®, add tortellini, broth, zucchini, mushrooms, tomatoes, Italian seasoning, garlic, and salt.

2 Close the lid; turn the knob to Sealing.

3 Press Manual or Pressure Cook button and adjust time to 4 minutes.

4 When the timer beeps, allow 5 minutes to naturally release the pressure, then remove the lid.

5 Stir in spinach and cream until combined. Remove to a serving plate, top with Parmesan, and serve.

PER SERVING

CALORIES: 593 | FAT: 27g | PROTEIN: 25g | SODIUM: 1,431mg
FIBER: 5g | CARBOHYDRATES: 61g | SUGAR: 8g

Egg Salad Sandwich

Egg salad sandwiches are delicious and satisfying, especially served on deliciously soft and pillowy bread. Packed with protein, this is a perfect quick and easy lunch that can be made in advance.

- **Hands-On Time: 5 minutes**
- **Cook Time: 16 minutes**

Serves 1

1 cup water
2 large eggs
1 tablespoon mayonnaise
⅛ teaspoon dried chives
⅛ teaspoon yellow mustard
1/16 teaspoon dried dill
1/16 teaspoon seasoned salt
1/16 teaspoon ground
    black pepper
2 slices whole-wheat bread

QUICK SNACK IDEA

Instead of making it into a sandwich, use egg salad as a dip for crackers, assorted vegetables, chips, or in a lettuce wrap. It's easy to add some chopped vegetables to the salad to make it more substantial if you're avoiding carbs.

1 Pour water into Instant Pot® and add the trivet. Place eggs on trivet.

2 Close the lid; turn the knob to Sealing.

3 Press Manual or Pressure Cook button and adjust time to 2 minutes.

4 When the timer beeps, allow 14 minutes to naturally release the pressure, then remove the lid.

5 Immediately place eggs in an ice bath; cool 10 minutes. Peel and cut in half, then remove the yolks to a small bowl.

6 Using a fork or whisk, break up egg yolks until very fine and crumbly. Mix in mayonnaise, chives, mustard, dill, seasoned salt, and pepper until smooth.

7 Mince egg whites and fold into yolk mixture. Spread mixture between 2 slices of bread and cut into triangles. Transfer to a plate and serve.

PER SERVING

CALORIES: 409 | FAT: 21g | PROTEIN: 21g | SODIUM: 603mg
FIBER: 4g | CARBOHYDRATES: 29g | SUGAR: 4g

Parmesan-Mushroom Risotto with Peas

You won't be missing any meat with this beautiful bowl of creamy risotto packed with mushrooms and dotted with gorgeous green peas. It's a fancy yet easy full meal that you can enjoy for yourself anytime.

- **Hands-On Time: 5 minutes**
- **Cook Time: 28 minutes**

Serves 1

1 tablespoon butter
¾ teaspoon minced garlic
1 teaspoon dried onion flakes
1 cup sliced mushrooms
⅛ teaspoon ground
    black pepper
¼ teaspoon salt
⅛ teaspoon dried thyme
⅛ teaspoon dried basil
½ cup uncooked Arborio rice
1¼ cups vegetable broth
1½ tablespoons white wine
¼ cup frozen peas
¼ cup shredded vegetarian
    Parmesan cheese

1 On the Instant Pot®, press Sauté button and adjust to High.

2 Add butter, garlic, onion flakes, mushrooms, pepper, salt, thyme, and basil. Sauté about 3–5 minutes until the mushrooms are browned.

3 Add rice and stir 2–3 minutes until rice is toasted. Add broth and wine and deglaze the pot, scraping all the browned bits off the bottom of the pot. Press Cancel button to turn off the heat.

4 Close the lid; turn the knob to Sealing.

5 Press Manual or Pressure Cook button and adjust time to 10 minutes.

6 When the timer beeps, allow 10 minutes to naturally release the pressure, then remove the lid.

7 Stir in peas and Parmesan. Transfer to a bowl and serve.

PER SERVING

CALORIES: 607 | **FAT:** 17g | **PROTEIN:** 19g | **SODIUM:** 1,961mg
FIBER: 5g | **CARBOHYDRATES:** 91g | **SUGAR:** 6g

Easy Mac 'n' Cheese

This no-drain Instant Pot® macaroni and cheese recipe is crazy delicious and easy. The hassle of boiling an entire pot of water for a single serving of noodles often isn't worth it, which may make you reach for takeout or some other kind of fast food. This recipe is ideal for anyone who needs a delicious, easy comfort meal.

- **Hands-On Time: 5 minutes**
- **Cook Time: 10 minutes**

Serves 1

¾ cup water

¾ cup uncooked elbow macaroni

⅛ teaspoon salt

3 tablespoons heavy cream

1 tablespoon butter

3 drops hot sauce

2 tablespoons shredded Muenster or smoked Gouda cheese

½ cup shredded Cheddar cheese

1 To the Instant Pot®, add water, macaroni, and salt.

2 Close the lid; turn the knob to Sealing.

3 Press Manual or Pressure Cook button and adjust time to 3 minutes.

4 When the timer beeps, allow 3 minutes to naturally release the pressure, then remove the lid.

5 Stir the macaroni to break up any clumps. Add cream, butter, and hot sauce, and stir until butter is melted. Slowly add in Muenster and Cheddar and stir until completely melted. If needed, turn on Sauté mode about 30–60 seconds to melt the cheese. Transfer to a bowl and serve.

PER SERVING

CALORIES: 701 | FAT: 48g | PROTEIN: 24g | SODIUM: 798mg
FIBER: 2g | CARBOHYDRATES: 35g | SUGAR: 2g

Angel Hair Margherita Pasta

Juicy summer tomatoes, fresh mozzarella, and garden-fresh basil combine with light angel hair pasta for one of the simplest and freshest meals you can make. The best thing is that it cooks in only 2 minutes, making it a great lunchtime option.

- **Hands-On Time: 5 minutes**
- **Cook Time: 2 minutes**

Serves 1

1 cup vegetable broth
¼ teaspoon minced garlic
1 tablespoon butter
½ teaspoon dried onion flakes
1/16 teaspoon crushed
    red pepper flakes
¼ teaspoon salt
3 ounces uncooked angel
    hair pasta, broken in half
1 cup chopped tomatoes
1 tablespoon olive oil
¼ cup chopped fresh
    mozzarella cheese
1 tablespoon vegetarian
    shredded Parmesan cheese
1 tablespoon chopped
    fresh basil

1 To the Instant Pot®, add broth, garlic, butter, onion flakes, red pepper flakes, and salt.

2 Layer pasta in a crisscross pattern over the liquid to reduce clumping. Top with tomatoes.

3 Close the lid; turn the knob to Sealing.

4 Press Manual or Pressure Cook button and adjust time to 2 minutes.

5 When the timer beeps, immediately turn the knob from Sealing to Venting, then remove the lid.

6 Stir the pasta to break up any clumps. Add oil and mozzarella chunks and toss to combine.

7 Transfer to a serving plate and top with Parmesan and basil. Serve immediately.

PER SERVING

CALORIES: 699 | FAT: 32g | PROTEIN: 23g | SODIUM: 1,705mg
FIBER: 5g | CARBOHYDRATES: 76g | SUGAR: 10g

Mushroom Stroganoff with Egg Noodles

Mushrooms and egg noodles cook together in a beautifully creamy and flavorful sauce for this super-quick meal! Feel free to use any assortment of mushrooms (up to 3 cups) in this recipe.

- **Hands-On Time: 5 minutes**
- **Cook Time: 10 minutes**

Serves 1

1 tablespoon butter
2 cups sliced mushrooms
¼ teaspoon salt
⅛ teaspoon ground black pepper
⅛ teaspoon smoked paprika
¼ teaspoon dried thyme
½ tablespoon dried onion flakes
½ teaspoon minced garlic
½ teaspoon soy sauce
1½ cups vegetable broth
1½ cups uncooked egg noodles
¼ cup sour cream
¼ cup heavy cream

1 On the Instant Pot®, press Sauté button and adjust to High.

2 Add butter and cook about 2 minutes until slightly brown. Add mushrooms and sprinkle with salt, pepper, paprika, and thyme. Sear 3 minutes.

3 Add onion flakes, garlic, soy sauce, broth, and noodles. Deglaze the pot, scraping all the browned bits off the bottom of the pot. Press Cancel button to turn off the heat.

4 Close the lid; turn the knob to Sealing.

5 Press Manual or Pressure Cook button and adjust time to 5 minutes.

6 When the timer beeps, immediately turn the knob from Sealing to Venting, then remove the lid.

7 Stir in sour cream and heavy cream. Transfer to a bowl and serve immediately.

PER SERVING

CALORIES: 723 | **FAT:** 45g | **PROTEIN:** 17g | **SODIUM:** 1,988mg **FIBER:** 4g | **CARBOHYDRATES:** 60g | **SUGAR:** 12g

Cheese Tortellini with Tomato-Cream Sauce

Look for the small, fresh cheese tortellini that can be found in the refrigerated pasta section of the grocery store. These packages are small enough for one to two portions and easy to add to a soup, serve with a premade sauce, or toss with vegetables. Cooking them in the Instant Pot® helps you avoid having to boil a large pot of water.

- **Hands-On Time: 2 minutes**
- **Cook Time: 8 minutes**

Serves 1

1½ cups uncooked fresh cheese tortellini
½ cup vegetable broth
½ teaspoon sugar
½ teaspoon minced garlic
1 (8-ounce) can tomato sauce
2 tablespoons heavy cream
1 teaspoon chopped fresh basil

1 To the Instant Pot®, add tortellini, broth, sugar, and garlic. Pour tomato sauce over tortellini and do not stir.

2 Close the lid; turn the knob to Sealing.

3 Press Manual or Pressure Cook button and adjust time to 3 minutes.

4 When the timer beeps, allow 5 minutes to naturally release the pressure, then remove the lid.

5 Stir in cream. Transfer to a bowl and top with basil. Serve.

PER SERVING

CALORIES: 669 | FAT: 21g | PROTEIN: 25g | SODIUM: 2,142mg
FIBER: 7g | CARBOHYDRATES: 93g | SUGAR: 14g

Quinoa and Corn Feta Salad

Vegetables and quinoa never looked so beautiful! This healthy meal is easy to make with quinoa left over from a larger family meal, or fresh for a single-portion make-ahead lunch or dinner. I like to purchase small bags of frozen edamame to keep as a healthy snack or to add to dishes like this.

- **Hands-On Time: 10 minutes**
- **Cook Time: 12 minutes**

Serves 1

½ cup uncooked quinoa, rinsed

1 cup water

½ cup fresh or frozen corn

½ cup shelled edamame

¼ cup drained and rinsed canned black beans

1 tablespoon lemon juice

1 tablespoon lime juice

2 tablespoons olive oil

½ tablespoon rice wine vinegar

1 tablespoon chopped cilantro

¼ teaspoon salt

1/16 teaspoon ground black pepper

¼ cup cherry tomatoes

3 tablespoons crumbled feta cheese

1 To the Instant Pot®, add quinoa and water.

2 Close the lid; turn the knob to Sealing.

3 Press Manual or Pressure Cook button and adjust time to 2 minutes.

4 When the timer beeps, allow 10 minutes to naturally release the pressure, then remove the lid.

5 Stir in corn, edamame, and beans. Take the Instant Pot® liner out of the base and let stand 8 minutes to cool quinoa and warm the corn, edamame, and beans.

6 In a small bowl, whisk together lemon juice, lime juice, oil, vinegar, cilantro, salt, and pepper.

7 Add tomatoes and feta to quinoa mixture, then toss with the dressing. Transfer to a bowl and serve immediately or refrigerate and served chilled.

PER SERVING

CALORIES: 853 | FAT: 41g | PROTEIN: 32g | SODIUM: 910mg
FIBER: 18g | CARBOHYDRATES: 91g | SUGAR: 8g

Cheesy Au Gratin Potatoes

If you like a crispy topping on your cheesy potatoes, toss ½ cup crushed (unsweetened) cornflakes, bread crumbs, potato chips, or crushed croutons with 1 tablespoon melted butter and sprinkle over the cooked potatoes. Broil 3–5 minutes until crispy.

- **Hands-On Time: 10 minutes**
- **Cook Time: 87 minutes**

Serves 1

1 cup water
1 tablespoon butter
1 tablespoon all-purpose flour
¾ cup whole milk
1¼ cups shredded Cheddar cheese, divided
⅛ teaspoon ground black pepper
⅛ teaspoon salt
1 medium unpeeled russet potato, sliced into ⅛" circles

1 Grease a 6" cake pan. Set aside.

2 Pour water into Instant Pot® and add the trivet.

3 In a small saucepan over medium heat, melt butter and add flour to make a roux. Cook 1 minute, then slowly add milk, whisking constantly.

4 Turn off heat and slowly whisk in ½ cup Cheddar. Whisk in pepper and salt and set aside.

5 Spread 2 tablespoons cheese sauce in the bottom of prepared cake pan. Layer six potato slices on top of the sauce, then top with 2 tablespoons Cheddar, and then 2 tablespoons cheese sauce. Repeat layers until all the potato slices have been used. Top the last layer with remaining sauce and Cheddar. Cover pan with foil.

6 Place pan on trivet in Instant Pot®.

7 Close the lid; turn the knob to Sealing.

8 Press Manual or Pressure Cook button and adjust time to 85 minutes.

9 When the timer beeps, immediately turn the knob from Sealing to Venting, then remove the lid and carefully remove the pan. Let stand 10 minutes and then serve.

PER SERVING

CALORIES: 980 | FAT: 57g | PROTEIN: 45g | SODIUM: 1,302mg
FIBER: 4g | CARBOHYDRATES: 54g | SUGAR: 12g

Easy Vegetable Ramen Stir-Fry

If it's packed full of vegetables, it's got to be healthy, right? I love making this meal by using up any odds and ends I find in the refrigerator and pantry. Everything tastes better mixed up with ramen noodles, even vegetables!

- **Hands-On Time: 5 minutes**
- **Cook Time: 1 minute**

Serves 1

1 (3-ounce) package vegetarian ramen noodle soup, soy sauce flavor
1 cup water
½ cup broccoli florets
¼ cup minced carrots
¼ cup frozen stir-fry vegetable mix
¼ teaspoon minced garlic
¼ teaspoon sesame oil
¼ teaspoon soy sauce

1 Break up the ramen noodles and scatter evenly in the Instant Pot®. Add remaining ingredients to the pot along with ½ teaspoon of the seasoning packet included with the ramen. Discard the remainder.

2 Close the lid; turn the knob to Sealing.

3 Press Manual or Pressure Cook button and adjust time to 1 minute.

4 When the timer beeps, immediately turn the knob from Sealing to Venting, then remove the lid. Fluff noodles and vegetables together, transfer to a serving plate, and serve.

PER SERVING

CALORIES: 398 | FAT: 15g | PROTEIN: 10g | SODIUM: 1,171mg
FIBER: 6g | CARBOHYDRATES: 59g | SUGAR: 3g

Butternut Squash Soup

Using precut butternut squash (available in the produce section of the grocery store) helps save time and money when cooking single portions, especially for this soup. See the note about blending small quantities in the Tomato Soup recipe (see Chapter 3).

- **Hands-On Time: 15 minutes**
- **Cook Time: 20 minutes**

Serves 1

1 tablespoon butter

2 tablespoons diced celery

2 tablespoons finely diced carrot

2 cups diced butternut squash

1 tablespoon dried onion flakes

1 cup water

¼ teaspoon plus ⅛ teaspoon ground cinnamon

¼ teaspoon plus ⅛ teaspoon salt

1 teaspoon chili powder

¼ cup heavy cream

1 On the Instant Pot®, press Sauté button and adjust to High. Add butter, celery, carrot, squash, and onion flakes. Sauté 5 minutes.

2 Stir in water, cinnamon, salt, and chili powder. Deglaze the pot, scraping all the browned bits off the bottom of the pot. Press Cancel button to turn off the heat.

3 Close the lid; turn the knob to Sealing.

4 Press Manual or Pressure Cook button and adjust time to 10 minutes.

5 When the timer beeps, allow 5 minutes to naturally release the pressure, then remove the lid and add cream.

6 Carefully transfer mixture to a blender and blend about 4 minutes until smooth. Alternatively, use an immersion blender directly in Instant Pot®. Ladle into a bowl and serve.

PER SERVING

CALORIES: 465 | FAT: 32g | PROTEIN: 5g | SODIUM: 1,006mg
FIBER: 8g | CARBOHYDRATES: 43g | SUGAR: 11g

Vegetable-Wild Rice Soup

Wild rice has a much sturdier bite to it than traditional white rice, which makes this soup so delicious and hearty that you won't miss the meat at all.

- **Hands-On Time: 5 minutes**
- **Cook Time: 55 minutes**

Serves 1

½ tablespoon dried
   onion flakes
½ teaspoon minced garlic
¼ cup diced carrots
¼ cup diced celery
¼ cup diced mushrooms
¼ cup fresh green beans,
   trimmed
¼ cup diced sweet potato
¼ cup uncooked
   wild rice blend
1 cup vegetable broth
¼ teaspoon salt
¼ teaspoon poultry seasoning
¼ teaspoon dried thyme
¼ cup heavy cream
1 tablespoon all-purpose flour

1 To the Instant Pot®, add all ingredients except cream and flour.

2 Close the lid; turn the knob to Sealing.

3 Press Manual or Pressure Cook button and adjust time to 45 minutes.

4 When the timer beeps, allow 5 minutes to naturally release the pressure, then remove the lid. Press Sauté button.

5 In a small bowl, whisk together cream and flour. When soup comes to a boil, stir in cream mixture. Cook about 3 minutes until thickened. Ladle into a bowl, then serve immediately.

PER SERVING

CALORIES: 451 | **FAT:** 22g | **PROTEIN:** 10g | **SODIUM:** 1,466mg
FIBER: 6g | **CARBOHYDRATES:** 55g | **SUGAR:** 10g

Spaghetti Squash with Lemon-Cream Sauce

This gorgeous dish is light yet savory and makes for an incredibly classy vegetarian dish.

- **Hands-On Time: 15 minutes**
- **Cook Time: 25 minutes**

Serves 1

1 cup water
1 small spaghetti squash
2 teaspoons lemon zest, divided
1 cup heavy cream
¼ teaspoon salt
1½ tablespoons lemon juice
⅛ teaspoon ground black pepper
1 teaspoon chopped fresh parsley
1 tablespoon shredded vegetarian Parmesan cheese

1. Pour water into Instant Pot® and add the trivet. Place spaghetti squash on trivet.

2. Close the lid; turn the knob to Sealing.

3. Press Manual or Pressure Cook button and adjust time to 20 minutes.

4. When the timer beeps, turn the knob from Sealing to Venting, remove the lid, and transfer squash to a cutting board. Cool 10 minutes.

5. Slice squash in half. (Cutting squash through the stem will result in shorter strands, while cutting crosswise through the center will result in longer strands.) Scoop out seeds from each half and discard. Using tongs or a fork, gently scrape and pull strands out of the shell into a strainer. Push squash against the sides of the strainer to remove as much liquid as possible, then measure 1 packed cup for this dish and reserve the rest for another use.

6. Drain and rinse out the Instant Pot® liner and place it back in the base. Press Sauté button and adjust to Low.

7. To the Instant Pot®, add 1 teaspoon lemon zest, cream, and salt. Stir to combine. Add squash and toss to coat. Press Cancel button to turn off the heat. Slowly stir in lemon juice and transfer to a serving bowl.

8. Swirl squash into a tall mound, then top with pepper, parsley, Parmesan, and remaining 1 teaspoon lemon zest. Serve.

PER SERVING

CALORIES: 940 | FAT: 86g | PROTEIN: 9g | SODIUM: 806mg
FIBER: 5g | CARBOHYDRATES: 30g | SUGAR: 16g

Simple Bowtie Pasta Marinara

This is a recipe my kids and I love because it's simple to make, and I always have the ingredients in the pantry. Make sure you use a high-quality marinara sauce with lots of flavor. If your pasta comes out tasting lackluster, add a little salt and some seasonings. Bowtie pasta is also referred to as farfalle.

- **Hands-On Time: 5 minutes**
- **Cook Time: 20 minutes**

Serves 1

1¼ cups uncooked bowtie
    pasta noodles
1 cup vegetable broth
1 cup marinara sauce
¼ cup shredded
    mozzarella cheese

1 To the Instant Pot®, add noodles and broth. Ensure all the noodles are submerged in broth. Pour marinara sauce on top of noodles. Do not stir.

2 Close the lid; turn the knob to Sealing.

3 Press Manual or Pressure Cook button and adjust time to 10 minutes.

4 When the timer beeps, allow 5 minutes to naturally release the pressure, then remove the lid.

5 Press Sauté button and adjust to High. Cook sauce about 5 minutes until reduced and thickened. Transfer to a plate, sprinkle with mozzarella, and serve.

PER SERVING

CALORIES: 569 | FAT: 9g | PROTEIN: 23g | SODIUM: 2,103mg
FIBER: 8g | CARBOHYDRATES: 93g | SUGAR: 20g

Spaghetti with Brown Butter and Mizithra Cheese

This meal has only a few ingredients, and I almost always have them on hand. Mizithra cheese is a harder cheese made from sheep's or goat's milk, but has a very mild and delicious flavor (it doesn't taste like traditional goat cheese). You can grate it and freeze it, or freeze it whole and use a microplane to grate the cheese directly from the freezer.

- **Hands-On Time: 3 minutes**
- **Cook Time: 5 minutes**

Serves 1

- 4 ounces uncooked spaghetti, broken in half
- 2 cups water
- 2 tablespoons grated mizithra cheese
- ⅛ teaspoon salt
- 1½ tablespoons brown butter

FREEZING CHEESE

You can freeze most cheeses, which is essential to avoid wasting ingredients you may not use all the time. I freeze every cheese used in this book with great success. If you freeze block cheese, consider cutting it into smaller cubes so you don't have to defrost the entire block before using it. Shredded cheese should be frozen as broken up as possible to avoid clumps. Cheeses like feta freeze and thaw quickly, so I usually sprinkle a little over my food straight from the freezer.

1 In the Instant Pot®, layer spaghetti in a crisscross pattern to reduce clumping. Pour in water.

2 Close the lid; turn the knob to Sealing.

3 Press Manual or Pressure Cook button and adjust time to 5 minutes.

4 When the timer beeps, immediately turn the knob from Sealing to Venting, then remove the lid and drain noodles.

5 Transfer spaghetti to a serving plate. Sprinkle cheese and salt over spaghetti, then drizzle with brown butter. Serve immediately.

PER SERVING

CALORIES: 694 | FAT: 29g | PROTEIN: 22g | SODIUM: 1,297mg
FIBER: 4g | CARBOHYDRATES: 86g | SUGAR: 4g

Rice, Beans, and Grains

Cooking rice, beans, and grains is one of the Instant Pot®'s specialties, because it requires no soaking and cooks everything perfectly. I love creating single portions of my favorite rice dishes because they don't end up dry and wasted in the refrigerator the next day. Rice and beans are staples around the world for good reason. They're extremely affordable and easy to make, they perfectly accompany almost any dish, and they also stand great on their own.

I've found that if you have the time, making beans from their dry state is the most affordable option that lets you control the flavor, salt, and amount of beans you'll have to enjoy in a dish or on their own.

The recipes in this chapter are incredibly easy to make in the Instant Pot® compared to traditional methods of preparation, which can be time consuming and difficult to execute successfully. Whatever recipes you make, I'm confident you'll be able to master each different kind of rice, bean, and grain in this chapter and start using (and eating!) them more freely.

Perfect Instant Pot® White Rice

Every Instant Pot® owner needs to know how to make simple white rice. The Instant Pot® cooks it quickly and perfectly every single time, so you'll never waste time making a single portion of rice on the stove ever again!

- **Hands-On Time: 1 minute**
- **Cook Time: 13 minutes**

Serves 1

½ cup uncooked long-grain white rice
¾ cup water
⅛ teaspoon salt

1 To the Instant Pot®, add all ingredients.

2 Close the lid; turn the knob to Sealing.

3 Press Manual or Pressure Cook button and adjust time to 3 minutes.

4 When the timer beeps, allow 10 minutes to naturally release the pressure, then remove the lid.

5 Fluff rice with a fork, transfer to a bowl, and serve.

PER SERVING

CALORIES: 337 | FAT: 1g | PROTEIN: 7g | SODIUM: 294mg
FIBER: 1g | CARBOHYDRATES: 74g | SUGAR: 0g

Jasmine Rice

Jasmine rice is one of the most popular varieties to make. The flavor is very mild and well suited to accompany any dish. I suggest pairing jasmine rice with your favorite saucy dish or grilled protein, or as a substitute for long-grain white rice.

- **Hands-On Time: 1 minute**
- **Cook Time: 13 minutes**

Serves 1

½ cup uncooked jasmine rice
¾ cup water
⅛ teaspoon salt

1 To the Instant Pot®, add all ingredients.

2 Close the lid; turn the knob to Sealing.

3 Press Manual or Pressure Cook button and adjust time to 3 minutes.

4 When the timer beeps, allow 10 minutes to naturally release the pressure, then remove the lid.

5 Fluff rice with a fork, transfer to a bowl, and serve.

PER SERVING

CALORIES: 320 | FAT: 0g | PROTEIN: 6g | SODIUM: 290mg
FIBER: 0g | CARBOHYDRATES: 72g | SUGAR: 0g

Perfect Instant Pot® Brown Rice

Brown rice provides more nutrients, fiber, and antioxidants than its white rice cousin. Because of that, I prefer to use brown rice almost anywhere white rice is served to pack more nutrition into my day.

- **Hands-On Time: 1 minute**
- **Cook Time: 25 minutes**

Serves 1

½ cup uncooked long-grain
    brown rice
¾ cup water
⅛ teaspoon salt

1 To the Instant Pot®, add rice, water, and salt.

2 Close the lid; turn the knob to Sealing.

3 Press Manual or Pressure Cook button and adjust time to 15 minutes.

4 When the timer beeps, allow 10 minutes to naturally release the pressure, then remove the lid.

5 Fluff rice with a fork, transfer to a bowl, and serve.

PER SERVING

CALORIES: 342 | FAT: 2g | PROTEIN: 7g | SODIUM: 296mg
FIBER: 3g | CARBOHYDRATES: 71g | SUGAR: 1g

Instant Pot® Wild Rice Blend

Plain wild rice is not only expensive (compared to other rice options), but it can also be difficult to find in stores. But I'm usually able to find affordable smaller bags of wild rice blends.

- **Hands-On Time: 1 minute**
- **Cook Time: 60 minutes**

Serves 1

½ cup uncooked wild
    rice blend
½ cup water
⅛ teaspoon salt

1 To the Instant Pot®, add rice, water, and salt.

2 Close the lid; turn the knob to Sealing.

3 Press Manual or Pressure Cook button and adjust time to 30 minutes.

4 When the timer beeps, allow a full natural pressure release, about 30 minutes. Then remove the lid.

5 Fluff rice with a fork, transfer to a bowl, and serve.

PER SERVING

CALORIES: 285 | FAT: 1g | PROTEIN: 12g | SODIUM: 295mg
FIBER: 5g | CARBOHYDRATES: 60g | SUGAR: 2g

Coconut Milk Rice

This rice is best served with a dish that complements coconut such as curry, teriyaki, or grilled meats and marinated vegetables.

- **Hands-On Time: 2 minutes**
- **Cook Time: 13 minutes**

Serves 1

½ cup uncooked jasmine rice
¾ cup canned unsweetened full-fat coconut milk
⅛ teaspoon salt
⅛ teaspoon sesame seeds

1 To the Instant Pot®, add rice, coconut milk, and salt.

2 Close the lid; turn the knob to Sealing.

3 Press Manual or Pressure Cook button and adjust time to 3 minutes.

4 When the timer beeps, allow 10 minutes to naturally release the pressure, then remove the lid.

5 Fluff rice with a fork and transfer to a bowl. Serve topped with sesame seeds.

PER SERVING

CALORIES: 655 | FAT: 34g | PROTEIN: 9g | SODIUM: 312mg
FIBER: 0g | CARBOHYDRATES: 77g | SUGAR: 0g

Instant Pot® Quinoa

Quinoa is an extremely healthy superfood that makes a great substitute for rice, meat, or pasta.

- **Hands-On Time: 1 minute**
- **Cook Time: 12 minutes**

Serves 1

½ cup uncooked quinoa, rinsed
1 cup water
⅛ teaspoon salt

1 To the Instant Pot®, add quinoa, water, and salt.

2 Close the lid; turn the knob to Sealing.

3 Press Manual or Pressure Cook button and adjust time to 2 minutes.

4 When the timer beeps, allow 10 minutes to naturally release the pressure, then remove the lid.

5 Fluff quinoa with a fork, transfer to a bowl, and serve.

PER SERVING

CALORIES: 312 | FAT: 5g | PROTEIN: 12g | SODIUM: 294mg
FIBER: 6g | CARBOHYDRATES: 55g | SUGAR: 0g

Wild Rice with Creamy Mushroom Sauce

You won't be able to stop taking bites of this incredibly cheesy and creamy wild rice. It's such a warm bowl of comfort that a single portion just might not be enough!

- **Hands-On Time: 5 minutes**
- **Cook Time: 53 minutes**

Serves 1

1 tablespoon butter

¼ cup finely diced mushrooms

2 teaspoons dried onion flakes

⅛ teaspoon salt

¼ teaspoon minced garlic

¼ cup uncooked wild rice blend

½ cup chicken broth

3 tablespoons shredded Parmesan cheese

3 tablespoons heavy cream

1 On the Instant Pot®, press Sauté button and adjust to High. Add butter, mushrooms, onion flakes, salt, garlic, and rice. Sauté 3 minutes.

2 Add broth and deglaze the pot, scraping all the browned bits off the bottom of the pot. Press Cancel button to turn off the heat.

3 Close the lid; turn the knob to Sealing.

4 Press Manual or Pressure Cook button and adjust time to 25 minutes.

5 When the timer beeps, allow a full natural pressure release, about 25 minutes, then remove the lid.

6 Stir in Parmesan and cream. Ladle into a bowl and serve.

PER SERVING

CALORIES: 479 | FAT: 31g | PROTEIN: 14g | SODIUM: 1,025mg
FIBER: 3g | CARBOHYDRATES: 35g | SUGAR: 4g

Homemade Refried Beans

I love topping these refried beans with Cheddar cheese, stuffing them inside a burrito, or using them as a chip dip. Since there's no lard in these refried beans, they're much healthier than the store-bought variety. If you prefer, you can add lard or bacon fat to taste.

- **Hands-On Time: 15 minutes**
- **Cook Time: 83 minutes**

Serves 1

½ cup dried pinto beans, rinsed and picked through

1½ cups water

1 tablespoon chopped green chilies

1 teaspoon minced garlic

¼ teaspoon ground cumin

¼ teaspoon chili powder

½ teaspoon dried oregano

1 tablespoon dried onion flakes

¼ teaspoon smoked paprika

¼ teaspoon ground cayenne pepper

½ teaspoon salt

1 To the Instant Pot®, add all ingredients except salt.

2 Close the lid; turn the knob to Sealing.

3 Press Manual or Pressure Cook button and adjust time to 65 minutes.

4 When the timer beeps, allow 10 minutes to naturally release the pressure, then remove the lid.

5 Press Sauté button and adjust to High. Cook beans about 5–8 minutes until most of the liquid has evaporated. If you prefer creamier refried beans, reduce for less time.

6 Add salt to beans. Using an immersion blender, carefully blend beans until creamy. Transfer to a bowl and serve.

PER SERVING

CALORIES: 362 | **FAT:** 1g | **PROTEIN:** 22g | **SODIUM:** 1,243mg
FIBER: 17g | **CARBOHYDRATES:** 67g | **SUGAR:** 5g

Cilantro-Lime Rice

The secret to this Cilantro-Lime Rice is to use both lemon *and* lime juice. You may use dried or fresh cilantro to make this dish. If you choose fresh, use 1 tablespoon minced. I give both options because often it's difficult to use an entire bunch of cilantro when cooking for one.

- **Hands-On Time: 5 minutes**
- **Cook Time: 13 minutes**

Serves 1

½ cup uncooked long-grain white rice
¾ cup water
1 teaspoon dried cilantro
2 tablespoons lime juice, divided
½ teaspoon salt
1 teaspoon lemon juice

HOW TO KEEP CILANTRO FRESH

Stand your fresh cilantro in a cup of water so that the stems are submerged, and loosely cover with a plastic bag. Keep the cup in the refrigerator and refresh the water every week. Use the cilantro as needed, and it'll stay fresh for weeks!

1 To the Instant Pot®, add rice, water, cilantro, 1 tablespoon lime juice, and salt.

2 Close the lid; turn the knob to Sealing.

3 Press Manual or Pressure Cook button and adjust time to 3 minutes.

4 When the timer beeps, allow 10 minutes to naturally release the pressure, then remove the lid.

5 Fluff rice with a fork and add remaining 1 tablespoon lime juice and lemon juice. Transfer to a bowl and serve immediately.

PER SERVING

CALORIES: 345 | FAT: 1g | PROTEIN: 7g | SODIUM: 1,166mg
FIBER: 1g | CARBOHYDRATES: 77g | SUGAR: 1g

Cowboy Caviar for One

As Cowboy Caviar is one of the most popular summertime recipes on my website, I knew a scaled-down version of it would be welcome! Cowboy Caviar, Texas Caviar, Corn and Black Bean Salsa or Salad—whatever you call it, this perfectly portioned favorite will be calling your name all summer long!

- **Hands-On Time: 8 minutes**
- **Cook Time: 3 minutes**

Serves 1

1 cup water
1 medium ear corn, husked
2 tablespoons chopped cilantro
2 tablespoons lime juice
2 tablespoons lemon juice
2 tablespoons olive oil
1½ tablespoons red wine vinegar
¼ teaspoon salt
⅛ teaspoon ground black pepper
¾ cup drained and rinsed canned black beans
2 tablespoons chopped green onion
¼ cup diced red bell pepper
½ cup diced avocado

1 Pour water into Instant Pot® and add the trivet. Place corn on trivet.

2 Close the lid; turn the knob to Sealing.

3 Press Manual or Pressure Cook button and adjust time to 3 minutes.

4 When the timer beeps, immediately turn the knob from Sealing to Venting, then remove the lid and carefully transfer corn to an ice bath.

5 In a medium bowl, combine cilantro, lime juice, lemon juice, oil, vinegar, salt, and black pepper. Add beans, green onion, and bell pepper, and stir.

6 Cut corn kernels off the cob and gently stir into bean mixture. Fold in avocado, transfer to a serving bowl and refrigerate at least 3 hours before serving.

PER SERVING

CALORIES: 722 | FAT: 45g | PROTEIN: 17g | SODIUM: 1,016mg
FIBER: 24g | CARBOHYDRATES: 67g | SUGAR: 10g

Bacon Black Beans

Making beans from their dried state is great for single-portion cooking, since you can control the amount you make without waste—a common problem with canned beans. It's also significantly more economical to use dried beans compared to canned.

- **Hands-On Time: 5 minutes**
- **Cook Time: 64 minutes**

Serves 1

1 slice uncooked thick-cut bacon, minced

1 tablespoon minced yellow onion

1 cup chicken broth

1 cup water

½ cup dried black beans, rinsed and picked through

¼ teaspoon minced garlic

1 bay leaf

¼ teaspoon ground cumin

¼ teaspoon dried oregano

1 teaspoon salt

1 On the Instant Pot®, press Sauté button and adjust to High. Add bacon and onion and sauté 4 minutes until bacon is crispy.

2 Add broth and water and deglaze the pot, scraping all the browned bits off the bottom of the pot. Add beans, garlic, bay leaf, cumin, oregano, and salt. Press Cancel button to turn off the heat.

3 Close the lid; turn the knob to Sealing.

4 Press Manual or Pressure Cook button and adjust time to 30 minutes.

5 When the timer beeps, allow a full natural pressure release, about 30 minutes, then remove the lid.

6 Stir beans, transfer to a bowl, and serve. Or, if you prefer a thicker consistency, leave beans in Instant Pot®. Press Sauté button and adjust to High. Cook 20 minutes until liquid is reduced, then press Cancel button to turn off the heat. Serve as desired.

PER SERVING

CALORIES: 587 | FAT: 23g | PROTEIN: 30g | SODIUM: 3,623mg
FIBER: 15g | CARBOHYDRATES: 63g | SUGAR: 4g

Spicy Pinto Beans

Depending on how much liquid you prefer in your pinto beans, you can reduce the final dish by cooking 5–10 minutes on Sauté mode to boil off any additional liquid and concentrate the flavors. The amount of salt in any bean recipe is up to you, but I tend to start conservatively and add as needed.

- **Hands-On Time: 5 minutes**
- **Cook Time: 75 minutes**

Serves 1

½ cup dried pinto beans, rinsed and picked through

1½ cups water

1 tablespoon chopped green chilies

1 teaspoon minced garlic

¼ teaspoon ground cumin

¼ teaspoon chili powder

½ teaspoon dried oregano

1 bay leaf

1 tablespoon dried onion flakes

¼ teaspoon smoked paprika

¼ teaspoon ground cayenne pepper

½ teaspoon salt

1 To the Instant Pot®, add all ingredients except salt.

2 Close the lid; turn the knob to Sealing.

3 Press Manual or Pressure Cook button and adjust time to 65 minutes.

4 When the timer beeps, allow 10 minutes to naturally release the pressure, then remove the lid.

5 Stir and remove bay leaf. Add salt, transfer to a bowl, and serve.

PER SERVING

CALORIES: 365 | FAT: 1g | PROTEIN: 22g | SODIUM: 1,243mg
FIBER: 17g | CARBOHYDRATES: 68g | SUGAR: 5g

Classic Parmesan Risotto

Traditional risotto takes an enormous amount of time and effort to create a perfectly creamy and tender dish. The Instant Pot® removes all the hassle to make an incredibly beautiful and simple meal or a large side dish for one.

- **Hands-On Time: 5 minutes**
- **Cook Time: 25 minutes**

Serves 1

1 tablespoon butter

1 teaspoon minced garlic

½ tablespoon dried onion flakes

⅛ teaspoon ground black pepper

¼ teaspoon salt

⅛ teaspoon dried thyme

¼ teaspoon Italian seasoning

½ cup uncooked Arborio rice

1¼ cups chicken broth

2 tablespoons white wine

½ cup shredded Parmesan cheese

½ cup heavy cream

1 teaspoon minced fresh parsley

1 On the Instant Pot®, press Sauté button and adjust to High.

2 Add butter, garlic, onion flakes, pepper, salt, thyme, Italian seasoning, and rice. Sauté about 3–5 minutes until the rice is toasted.

3 Add broth and wine and deglaze the pot, scraping all the browned bits off the bottom of the pot. Press Cancel button to turn off the heat.

4 Close the lid; turn the knob to Sealing.

5 Press Manual or Pressure Cook button and adjust time to 10 minutes.

6 When the timer beeps, allow 10 minutes to naturally release the pressure, then remove the lid.

7 Stir in Parmesan and cream and transfer to a serving bowl. Top with parsley and serve.

PER SERVING

CALORIES: 1,077 | FAT: 64g | PROTEIN: 27g | SODIUM: 2,460mg
FIBER: 3g | CARBOHYDRATES: 89g | SUGAR: 6g

Herb and Butter Rice-A-Roni

After talking to several people that regularly cook for one, I learned that Rice-A-Roni is a popular and staple side dish. Now it's even easier made in the Instant Pot®. If you prefer to make the entire box of rice, simply add it, double the water, and add the entire seasoning packet.

- **Hands-On Time: 5 minutes**
- **Cook Time: 15 minutes**

Serves 1

½ tablespoon butter

½ cup uncooked Herb & Butter Rice-A-Roni

¾ cup water

1 tablespoon seasoning from Rice-A-Roni seasoning packet

MAKE IT A MEAL

Add 1 cup diced chicken breast, chicken thighs, chicken tenderloin, or pork tenderloin to the rice and cook as directed. Serve with a side of vegetables and you've got a full meal that's ready to go in 30 minutes or less.

1 On the Instant Pot®, press Sauté button and adjust to High.

2 Add butter and Rice-A-Roni and toast 2 minutes, stirring constantly. Add water and press Cancel button to turn off the heat.

3 Close the lid; turn the knob to Sealing

4 Press Manual or Pressure Cook button and adjust time to 3 minutes.

5 When the timer beeps, allow 10 minutes to naturally release the pressure, then remove the lid.

6 Fluff rice with a fork and stir in seasoning. Transfer to a bowl and serve.

PER SERVING

CALORIES: 409 | **FAT:** 8g | **PROTEIN:** 8g | **SODIUM:** 1,199mg **FIBER:** 2g | **CARBOHYDRATES:** 80g | **SUGAR:** 3g

Brown Butter, Lemon, and Garlic Rice Pilaf

Pilaf is a rice that has been precooked or sautéed before steaming. To make this recipe using brown rice: Use all the same measurements for the ingredients, substituting long-grain brown rice for the white rice. Sauté as directed, but during the Pressure Cook step, adjust the cook time to 15 minutes. Proceed as directed. Serve this dish with a sprinkle of chopped parsley for color.

- **Hands-On Time: 6 minutes**
- **Cook Time: 9 minutes**

Serves 1

1 tablespoon butter
½ cup uncooked long-grain white rice
½ teaspoon minced garlic
¾ cup water
1 tablespoon lemon juice
½ teaspoon ground lemon pepper
1 tablespoon shredded Parmesan cheese

1 On the Instant Pot®, press Sauté button and adjust to High. Add butter and sauté about 4 minutes until golden and nutty smelling.

2 Add rice and garlic and sauté an additional 1–2 minutes until rice is toasted. Press Cancel button to turn off the heat.

3 Add water, lemon juice, and lemon pepper; deglaze the pot, scraping all the browned bits off the bottom of the pot.

4 Close the lid; turn the knob to Sealing.

5 Press Manual or Pressure Cook button and adjust time to 3 minutes.

6 When the timer beeps, allow 10 minutes to naturally release the pressure, then remove the lid.

7 Fluff rice with a fork, transfer to a bowl, top with Parmesan, and serve.

PER SERVING

CALORIES: 463 | FAT: 13g | PROTEIN: 9g | SODIUM: 149mg
FIBER: 1g | CARBOHYDRATES: 76g | SUGAR: 1g

Sweet and Smoky Baked Beans

Making "baked" beans in the Instant Pot® from scratch is incredibly easy and delicious! Most recipes for baked beans will call for a can of pork and beans or commercially made baked beans, but these are 100 percent homemade and some of the best you'll ever have. If you have some other beans on hand that you prefer, you may replace the great northern beans with your favorite variety.

- **Hands-On Time: 5 minutes**
- **Cook Time: 15 minutes**

Serves 1

3 tablespoons real bacon crumbles
1 tablespoon dried onion flakes
½ teaspoon minced garlic
1 (15.5-ounce) can great northern beans, drained and rinsed
½ cup apple juice
½ cup water
1 tablespoon ketchup
2 tablespoons barbecue sauce
½ tablespoon soy sauce
1½ tablespoons brown sugar
½ tablespoon molasses

1 To the Instant Pot®, add all ingredients and stir.

2 Close the lid; turn the knob to Sealing.

3 Press Manual or Pressure Cook button and adjust time to 10 minutes.

4 When the timer beeps, immediately turn the knob from Sealing to Venting, then remove the lid.

5 Press Sauté button and adjust to High. Cook 5 minutes to reduce sauce, then ladle into a bowl and serve.

PER SERVING

CALORIES: 875 | FAT: 8g | PROTEIN: 45g | SODIUM: 2,435mg
FIBER: 24g | CARBOHYDRATES: 162g | SUGAR: 63g

Pot-in-Pot Black Beans and Rice

Two side dishes in one! Black beans and seasoning cook above the rice in their own dish so that you'll be able to enjoy both dishes without cooking twice. This is a smart and easy way to utilize your Instant Pot® on the side while you prepare another main dish to enjoy with this recipe.

- **Hands-On Time: 5 minutes**
- **Cook Time: 14 minutes**

Serves 1

½ cup uncooked long-grain white rice
¾ cup chicken broth
⅛ teaspoon minced garlic
½ cup drained and rinsed canned black beans
⅛ teaspoon dried cilantro
⅛ teaspoon ground cumin
⅛ teaspoon dried oregano
⅛ teaspoon garlic salt
⅛ teaspoon chili powder

COOKING POT-IN-POT

You can cook pot-in-pot dishes where the two components cook for roughly the same time, or if one of the components is forgiving. You'll need to calculate foods that you want to cook together and then use the lowest common denominator of time. Other PIP recipes in this book are the potatoes and egg for my Classic Potato Salad (see Chapter 4) or the Cheesy Cajun Shrimp and Grits recipe (see Chapter 8).

1 To the Instant Pot®, add rice, broth, and garlic. Add the trivet.

2 In a small pressure-proof bowl, combine beans, cilantro, cumin, oregano, salt, and chili powder. Place bowl on trivet.

3 Close the lid; turn the knob to Sealing.

4 Press Manual or Pressure Cook button and adjust time to 4 minutes.

5 When the timer beeps, allow 10 minutes to naturally release the pressure, then remove the lid.

6 Carefully remove bowl of beans to a serving dish, then remove the trivet. Fluff rice with a fork and serve alongside beans.

PER SERVING

CALORIES: 458 | FAT: 1g | PROTEIN: 15g | SODIUM: 1,222mg
FIBER: 10g | CARBOHYDRATES: 95g | SUGAR: 1g

11

Desserts for One

Between September and October of every year, I push my eager cart by the case of pumpkin pies at Costco and tell myself I *do not* need to buy one. But week after week, I'm there…as the pumpkin pies will me to take one home with me. Eventually, I always cave and give in to satisfying that intense craving for just a *single slice* of pumpkin pie. I then shamefully proceed to lug a giant pumpkin pie into my oversized cart, devour every bite of the one-sixteenth of the pie, and then get tired of it.

Single-serving and small-batch desserts are perfect for that small after-dinner treat, or to satisfy a craving (at *any* time of day) without having to make (or buy!) an entire pan of something that might go to waste. These recipes are also amazing to accommodate friends or guests who may have certain dietary restrictions and need an alternative at a gathering. Have a friend who's having a bad day but don't want to make an entire cake? Why not brighten their day with a mini Molten Chocolate Lava Cake or personal Vanilla Bean Crème Brûlée? Everyone needs a little sweet treat now and then to satisfy that sweet tooth (why do my cravings always happen at nine p.m.?!). Whenever your hunger strikes, I know you'll love the simple and delicious single-serve desserts in this chapter.

Crustless Pumpkin Pie Bites

Perfectly portioned bites of pumpkin pie help satisfy the craving any time of year! This recipe creates three Crustless Pumpkin Pie Bites, equivalent to about one slice of pie. Since this recipe is crustless, it's also gluten-free. Make sure to use the leftover pumpkin to make Two-Layered Creamy Pumpkin Yogurt (see Chapter 2).

- **Hands-On Time: 5 minutes**
- **Cook Time: 25 minutes**

Serves 1

¼ cup pumpkin puree
3 tablespoons sugar
¼ cup heavy cream
1 large egg
¼ teaspoon pumpkin pie spice
1⁄16 teaspoon salt
1 cup water
2 tablespoons sweetened whipped cream

1 Grease three cups of a silicone egg bites mold. Set aside.

2 In a small bowl, whisk together pumpkin, sugar, heavy cream, egg, pumpkin pie spice, and salt until combined.

3 Equally divide the mixture among prepared egg bite mold cups. Cover tightly with foil.

4 Pour water into Instant Pot® and add the trivet.

5 Place mold on trivet. Alternatively, place the mold on a silicone sling and lower into the Instant Pot® (in lieu of the trivet).

6 Close the lid; turn the knob to Sealing.

7 Press Manual or Pressure Cook button and adjust time to 20 minutes.

8 When the timer beeps, allow 5 minutes to naturally release the pressure, then remove the lid.

9 Allow pie bites to cool to room temperature, then refrigerate 4–8 hours until set.

10 Remove foil, invert pie bites onto a plate, and enjoy with whipped cream.

PER SERVING

CALORIES: 484 | FAT: 27g | PROTEIN: 9g | SODIUM: 243mg
FIBER: 3g | CARBOHYDRATES: 50g | SUGAR: 43g

Gooey Chocolate Chip Cookie Sundae

Nothing's better than a warm, ooey-gooey chocolate chip cookie topped with cold vanilla bean ice cream and nuts. This single-serve recipe is the perfect midnight indulgence, and you won't even have to make an entire batch of cookie dough.

- **Hands-On Time: 5 minutes**
- **Cook Time: 25 minutes**

Serves 1

1½ tablespoons butter, melted
1 tablespoon brown sugar
1 tablespoon granulated sugar
1 large egg yolk
½ teaspoon vanilla extract
⅓ cup all-purpose flour
⅛ teaspoon baking soda
1/16 teaspoon salt
1 tablespoon mini semisweet chocolate chips
1 cup water
¼ cup vanilla bean ice cream
1 tablespoon chopped pecans
1 tablespoon chocolate syrup

COOKIE VARIATIONS

Try replacing 1 tablespoon of the flour with cocoa powder to make a chocolate cookie, and feel free to add up to 2 tablespoons of extra mix-ins to the cookie dough. I suggest coconut, white chocolate chips, oats, mini candies, or dried fruit.

1 Grease an 8-ounce ramekin. Set aside.

2 In a small bowl, combine butter with brown sugar and granulated sugar until dissolved.

3 Add egg yolk and vanilla and mix until smooth.

4 Add flour, baking soda, and salt; combine to make a dough. Mix in chocolate chips.

5 Scrape dough into prepared ramekin and press into the bottom of the ramekin. Cover with foil.

6 Pour water into Instant Pot® and add the trivet. Place ramekin on trivet.

7 Close the lid; turn the knob to Sealing.

8 Press Manual or Pressure Cook button and adjust time to 20 minutes.

9 When the timer beeps, allow 5 minutes to naturally release the pressure, then remove the lid.

10 Carefully remove ramekin from the pot. Remove foil and cool 3–5 minutes.

11 Top warm cookie with ice cream, pecans, and chocolate syrup. Serve immediately.

PER SERVING

CALORIES: 695 | FAT: 33g | PROTEIN: 10g | SODIUM: 407mg
FIBER: 3g | CARBOHYDRATES: 86g | SUGAR: 46g

Berry Almond "Crisp"

Frozen berries are sold in affordable smaller bags in the grocery store, making this an accessible and inexpensive dessert to make in a single serving.

- **Hands-On Time: 8 minutes**
- **Cook Time: 35 minutes**

Serves 1

¾ cup frozen berry mix
½ teaspoon almond extract
2 tablespoons granulated sugar
½ tablespoon cornstarch
1 tablespoon cold butter, cut up
1 tablespoon brown sugar
$\frac{1}{16}$ teaspoon ground cinnamon
$\frac{1}{16}$ teaspoon nutmeg
1½ tablespoons all-purpose flour
1½ tablespoons rolled oats
1 cup water
¼ cup vanilla ice cream

1 In a small bowl, toss together berries, almond extract, granulated sugar, and cornstarch. Pour into an 8-ounce ramekin.

2 In a separate small bowl, using a fork, combine butter, brown sugar, cinnamon, nutmeg, flour, and oats until mixture resembles large crumbs. Crumble over berry mixture and cover with foil.

3 Pour water into Instant Pot® and add the trivet. Place ramekin on trivet.

4 Close the lid; turn the knob to Sealing.

5 Press Manual or Pressure Cook button and adjust time to 25 minutes.

6 When the timer beeps, allow 10 minutes to naturally release the pressure, then remove the lid.

7 Carefully remove ramekin from the Instant Pot®, then remove foil and let cool 5 minutes. Top with ice cream and serve immediately.

PER SERVING

CALORIES: 463 | FAT: 15g | PROTEIN: 4g | SODIUM: 30mg
FIBER: 6g | CARBOHYDRATES: 78g | SUGAR: 53g

Easy Mango Sticky Rice

Why spend $10 on a restaurant dessert that can be made for pennies at home? This Easy Mango Sticky Rice features ripe, fresh mangoes, a sweet and creamy coconut sauce, and a sticky, delicious base of rice. Make sure to use canned full-fat coconut milk and shake the can before using.

- **Hands-On Time: 8 minutes**
- **Cook Time: 15 minutes**

Serves 1

Sticky Rice
½ cup uncooked jasmine rice
¾ cup canned unsweetened full-fat coconut milk
⅛ teaspoon salt

Coconut Sauce
½ cup canned unsweetened full-fat coconut milk
4 teaspoons sugar
1⁄16 teaspoon salt
½ tablespoon cornstarch
½ tablespoon cold water

For Serving
½ cup ripe mango slices, chilled
½ teaspoon toasted sesame seeds

NOT A FAN OF MANGO?

If you don't care for mango try using fresh pineapple, guava, peaches, papaya, or even fresh berries instead! Top the rice with toasted coconut in place of sesame seeds, if desired.

1 To the Instant Pot®, add all Sticky Rice ingredients.

2 Close the lid; turn the knob to Sealing.

3 Press Manual or Pressure Cook button and adjust time to 3 minutes.

4 When the timer beeps, allow 10 minutes to naturally release the pressure, then remove the lid.

5 While the rice is cooking, make the Coconut Sauce. In a small saucepan over medium heat, combine coconut milk, sugar, and salt.

6 In a small bowl, mix together cornstarch and cold water to make a slurry. When coconut milk mixture comes to a boil, whisk in the slurry about 1–2 minutes until thickened. Remove from heat and allow to cool to room temperature.

7 Add ¼ cup Coconut Sauce to the rice in the Instant Pot® and stir to combine. Replace the lid and let cool 10 minutes.

8 To serve, spoon rice into a bowl and arrange mango slices over rice. Pour remaining coconut sauce over the top and sprinkle with sesame seeds. May be served warm or cold.

PER SERVING

CALORIES: 1,012 | FAT: 58g | PROTEIN: 13g | SODIUM: 471mg
FIBER: 2g | CARBOHYDRATES: 113g | SUGAR: 28g

Stuffed Baked Apple à la Mode

Slice open this super-stuffed apple, and the caramel sauce spills over the entire dish, melting into the vanilla ice cream and giving you all the flavors and textures of a caramel apple pie without the fuss and calories.

- **Hands-On Time: 6 minutes**
- **Cook Time: 12 minutes**

Serves 1

1 medium Honeycrisp apple
1 tablespoon brown sugar
1 tablespoon butter
½ teaspoon ground cinnamon
1 tablespoon chopped pecans
1 tablespoon sweetened
    dried cranberries
1 cup water
¼ cup vanilla ice cream

APPLE TIPS

The size and sweetness of apples vary greatly. If you decide to use a tarter apple such as a Granny Smith, I recommend adding an extra tablespoon of brown sugar to the apple. Try to choose apples that are free from bruises or cuts and that have a sturdy base.

1 Core apple and scrape out center to create a cavity in the middle about 1" in diameter.

2 In a small bowl, mix together brown sugar, butter, cinnamon, pecans, and cranberries into a paste. Scoop paste into apple and cover the top with a small piece of foil.

3 Pour water into Instant Pot® and add the trivet. Place apple on trivet.

4 Close the lid; turn the knob to Sealing.

5 Press Manual or Pressure Cook button and adjust time to 7 minutes.

6 When the timer beeps, allow 5 minutes to naturally release the pressure, then remove the lid.

7 Using tongs, carefully remove apple from the Instant Pot® and transfer to a bowl. Let cool 5 minutes.

8 Top with ice cream and serve immediately.

PER SERVING

CALORIES: 392 | **FAT:** 19g | **PROTEIN:** 2g | **SODIUM:** 31mg
FIBER: 6g | **CARBOHYDRATES:** 53g | **SUGAR:** 43g

Cinnamon-Vanilla Rice Pudding

This recipe is one of the most popular ones from my website, scaled down here to give you a perfect single portion. You'll be making this over and over again to enjoy for breakfast or dessert! If you like raisins in your rice pudding, add them to the rice with the sugar.

- **Hands-On Time: 7 minutes**
- **Cook Time: 18 minutes**

Serves 1

½ cup uncooked long-grain white rice

1 cup water

¹⁄₁₆ teaspoon salt

2½ tablespoons sugar

1 cup whole milk, divided

1 large egg

½ tablespoon butter

½ tablespoon vanilla extract

2 tablespoons heavy cream

⅛ teaspoon ground cinnamon

1 To the Instant Pot®, add rice, water, and salt.

2 Close the lid; turn the knob to Sealing.

3 Press Manual or Pressure Cook button and adjust time to 3 minutes.

4 When the timer beeps, allow 10 minutes to naturally release the pressure, then remove the lid.

5 Fluff rice, then add sugar and stir to dissolve. Press Sauté button and adjust to Low. Whisk in ½ cup milk and bring to a low simmer.

6 In a liquid measuring cup, measure remaining ½ cup milk and whisk together with egg until completely combined.

7 While whisking, pour egg mixture into the pot until completely incorporated. Whisk about 5 minutes until thickened. Press Cancel button to turn off the heat.

8 Stir in butter, vanilla, and cream. Scoop into a bowl and serve with a sprinkle of cinnamon.

PER SERVING

CALORIES: 847 | FAT: 28g | PROTEIN: 22g | SODIUM: 335mg
FIBER: 1g | CARBOHYDRATES: 119g | SUGAR: 45g

Single-Layer Carrot Cake with Cream Cheese Frosting

Nothing's better than this incredibly dense carrot cake that's chock-full of carrots, nuts, coconut, and pineapple. This cake is not a lightly spiced cake with flecks of carrot. Get ready for the best carrot cake you've ever had, in a manageable portion! Top this cake with additional coconut, nuts, and/or pineapple if desired.

- **Hands-On Time: 15 minutes**
- **Cook Time: 75 minutes**

Serves 1

Carrot Cake
¼ cup granulated sugar
¼ cup brown sugar
2 tablespoons canola oil
1 large egg, lightly beaten
1 teaspoon vanilla extract
½ cup all-purpose flour
¾ teaspoon ground cinnamon
⅛ teaspoon ground nutmeg
⅛ teaspoon ground cloves
½ teaspoon baking soda
1 cup shredded carrots
½ cup pecans
⅓ cup chopped pineapple
¼ cup sweetened
    shredded coconut
1 cup water

Cream Cheese Frosting
4 ounces cream cheese,
    softened
3 tablespoons butter
1½ teaspoons vanilla extract
¹⁄₁₆ teaspoon salt
2 cups confectioners' sugar

1 Grease a 6" cake pan. Set aside.

2 In a medium bowl, combine granulated sugar, brown sugar, and oil. Add egg and vanilla and stir until combined.

3 Sift in flour, cinnamon, nutmeg, cloves, and baking soda. Stir to combine. The batter will be very thick.

4 Add carrots, pecans, pineapple, and coconut. Stir well, then let rest 5 minutes to allow the moisture from the carrots and pineapple to soften the batter.

5 Pour batter into prepared cake pan and cover tightly with foil.

6 Pour water into Instant Pot® and add the trivet. Place pan on trivet.

7 Close the lid; turn the knob to Sealing.

8 Press Manual or Pressure Cook button and adjust time to 60 minutes.

9 When the timer beeps, allow 15 minutes to naturally release the pressure, then remove the lid.

10 Carefully remove pan and let cool 15 minutes before placing in the refrigerator at least 5 hours, preferably overnight.

11 To make the Cream Cheese Frosting, in a medium bowl, combine all ingredients except confectioners' sugar. Whisk together or blend using an electric mixer until smooth.

12 Add confectioners' sugar 1 cup at a time. Incorporate each cup before adding the next. (If needed, add milk or cream to thin.)

13 Remove cake from pan and frost with Cream Cheese Frosting. Serve.

PER SERVING

CALORIES: 2,962 | **FAT:** 138g | **PROTEIN:** 27g | **SODIUM:** 1,417mg
FIBER: 14g | **CARBOHYDRATES:** 395g | **SUGAR:** 324g

Vanilla Bean Crème Brûlée

Crème brûlée is traditionally baked in a bain-marie (water bath) in the oven for an hour. With the Instant Pot®, it couldn't be easier to make a single ramekin of creamy crème brûlée in less than half the time. Feel free to use the same amount of vanilla extract if you don't have vanilla bean paste on hand.

- **Hands-On Time: 10 minutes**
- **Cook Time: 20 minutes**

Serves 1

½ cup heavy cream
½ teaspoon vanilla bean paste
2 large egg yolks
2 tablespoons sugar, divided
1 cup water
3 whole raspberries

1   In a small saucepan over medium-high heat, combine cream and vanilla bean paste until steaming. Do not boil. Remove from heat.

2   In a small bowl, whisk egg yolks and 1 table-spoon sugar until light and smooth. While whisking, slowly pour hot cream into egg yolks and whisk to combine. Pour cream mixture through a fine-mesh strainer into an 8-ounce ramekin. Cover with foil.

3   Pour water into Instant Pot® and add the trivet. Place ramekin on trivet. Close the lid; turn the knob to Sealing. Press Manual or Pressure Cook button and adjust time to 10 minutes. Then press Pressure Level button and adjust to Low Pressure. If your Instant Pot® does not have a Low Pressure button, adjust the time to 8 minutes.

4   When the timer beeps, allow 10 minutes to naturally release the pressure, then remove the lid. Remove ramekin to cooling rack. Let cool and then refrigerate 6–8 hours.

5   To serve, remove foil. Sprinkle remaining 1 tablespoon sugar over the top of the crème brûlée. Using a kitchen torch, quickly torch the sugar in small circles until sugar is completely caramelized. Cool 1 minute, then top with raspberries and serve.

PER SERVING

CALORIES: 624 | FAT: 50g | PROTEIN: 8g | SODIUM: 61mg
FIBER: 0g | CARBOHYDRATES: 31g | SUGAR: 30g

Japanese Crème Caramel (Purin)

Purin ("poo-lrin"), or Japanese crème caramel custard pudding, is so popular in Japan that you can even find an emoji for it on your phone keyboard! Unlike Mexican flan, this recipe is very soft, smooth, and light. It's traditionally steamed in a circular plateau-shaped mold, but a regular 6- or 8-ounce ramekin will do.

- **Hands-On Time: 10 minutes**
- **Cook Time: 34 minutes**

Serves 1

4 tablespoons sugar, divided

1 cup plus 2 tablespoons and 1 teaspoon water, divided

½ cup whole milk

1 large egg yolk

½ teaspoon vanilla extract

1 tablespoon sweetened whipped cream

1 maraschino cherry

1   To a small saucepan over medium heat, add 3 tablespoons sugar and 2 tablespoons water. Tilt the pot and swirl to combine the mixture—do not stir—and cook about 6 minutes until dark amber in color and caramelized. Do not overcook.

2   Remove from heat and carefully add 1 teaspoon water to the caramel to thin. Quickly and carefully pour the hot caramel into an 8-ounce ramekin and set aside.

3   In a separate small saucepan over medium heat, heat milk until steaming, then remove from heat. In a small bowl, whisk egg yolk and remaining 1 tablespoon sugar until creamy. Slowly pour hot milk mixture into egg yolk mixture while constantly whisking. Whisk in vanilla, then pour mixture over caramel in the ramekin and cover with foil.

4   Pour remaining 1 cup water into Instant Pot® and add the trivet. Place ramekin on trivet.

5   Close the lid; turn the knob to Sealing.

6   Press Manual or Pressure Cook button and adjust time to 13 minutes. Then press Pressure Level button and adjust to Low Pressure. If your Instant Pot® does not have a Low Pressure button, adjust the time to 9 minutes.

7 When the timer beeps, allow 15 minutes to naturally release the pressure, then remove the lid.

8 Carefully remove ramekin from the Instant Pot® and let cool to room temperature. Then refrigerate 6–8 hours or overnight.

9 When ready to serve, slide a wet knife around the edges of custard, then invert onto a plate. Serve with whipped cream and cherry.

PER SERVING

CALORIES: 416 | **FAT:** 12g | **PROTEIN:** 10g | **SODIUM:** 112mg
FIBER: 0g | **CARBOHYDRATES:** 65g | **SUGAR:** 65g

Bread Pudding with Buttered Rum Sauce

This recipe was inspired by a highly indulgent bread pudding recipe served at a luxury hotel in downtown Salt Lake City. This single portion is absolute perfection.

- Hands-On Time: 10 minutes
- Cook Time: 40 minutes

Serves 1

Bread Pudding

1 large egg

¾ cup heavy cream

¼ cup granulated sugar

2 teaspoons vanilla extract

4 slices Texas Toast bread, dried overnight and diced into 1" cubes

⅛ teaspoon ground cinnamon

1 cup water

Buttered Rum Sauce

2 tablespoons granulated sugar

1 tablespoon apple juice

1½ tablespoons brown sugar

2 tablespoons heavy cream

¼ teaspoon rum extract

⅛ teaspoon vanilla extract

2 tablespoons butter

1 Grease a 6" cake pan. Set aside.

2 In a small saucepan over medium heat, whisk together egg, ¾ cup cream, and ¼ cup granulated sugar until mixture starts to bubble slightly on the sides and steam. Do not boil. Add 2 teaspoons vanilla and remove from heat.

3 Arrange bread pieces in prepared cake pan, then pour cream mixture over the top and let soak 5 minutes. Sprinkle cinnamon on top. Cover pan tightly with foil.

4 Pour water into Instant Pot® and add the trivet. Place pan on trivet.

5 Close the lid; turn the knob to Sealing.

6 Press Manual or Pressure Cook button and adjust time to 35 minutes.

7 Prepare the Buttered Rum Sauce: In a separate small saucepan over medium heat, combine 2 tablespoons granulated sugar, apple juice, brown sugar, and 2 tablespoons cream. Boil 5 minutes. Remove from heat, then add rum extract, ⅛ teaspoon vanilla, and butter, whisking constantly. Set aside.

8 When the timer beeps on the Instant Pot®, allow 5 minutes to naturally release the pressure, then remove the lid.

9 Remove pan, remove foil, and serve immediately with Buttered Rum Sauce.

PER SERVING

CALORIES: 1,819 | FAT: 103g | PROTEIN: 25g | SODIUM: 941mg
FIBER: 5g | CARBOHYDRATES: 184g | SUGAR: 113g

Brown Butter–Cinnamon Rice Crispy Treat

This easy recipe uses the Sauté feature on the Instant Pot® to elevate a childhood favorite into a delectable small bite.

- **Hands-On Time: 4 minutes**
- **Cook Time: 6 minutes**

Serves 1

½ tablespoon butter
½ cup mini marshmallows
⅛ teaspoon vanilla extract
1⁄16 teaspoon ground cinnamon
1 cup crispy rice cereal
1⁄16 teaspoon coarse sea salt

CEREAL BARS

Try using a different type of cereal for a fun and different treat. Our favorites are Cocoa Pebbles or Fruity Pebbles, or anything that has peanut butter or marshmallows!

1 Lightly grease a medium bowl or line a small baking sheet with waxed paper.

2 On the Instant Pot®, press Sauté button and adjust to Medium. Add butter and cook about 4 minutes until slightly golden and browned.

3 Adjust the Instant Pot® Sauté setting to Low and add marshmallows. When melted, press Cancel button to turn off the heat and add vanilla and cinnamon. Stir to combine, then add cereal and mix until completely combined.

4 Scrape mixture into prepared bowl or onto lined baking sheet. Lightly pat down to shape. Immediately sprinkle with salt, then cool at least 10 minutes and serve.

PER SERVING

CALORIES: 240 | **FAT:** 6g | **PROTEIN:** 2g | **SODIUM:** 269mg
FIBER: 0g | **CARBOHYDRATES:** 45g | **SUGAR:** 17g

Molten Chocolate Lava Cake

Finding a chocolate lava cake recipe without using tons of butter, separating eggs, and loads of calories is next to impossible. This recipe is a perfect indulgence that's simple, easy, and super chocolatey! Adjust the cooking time 5–9 minutes, depending on how much "lava" flow you like in the middle of the cake.

- **Hands-On Time: 5 minutes**
- **Cook Time: 8 minutes**

Serves 1

½ cup semisweet
   chocolate chips
2 tablespoons butter
½ cup confectioners' sugar
1 large egg
¼ teaspoon vanilla extract
1 tablespoon all-purpose flour
½ tablespoon cocoa powder
1 cup water

TRY THIS!
Swap out regular chocolate chips for white, peanut butter, dark, or caramel chips for a yummy flavor variation.

1 In a medium microwave-safe bowl, combine chocolate chips and butter. Microwave in 10-second intervals until completely melted.

2 Add sugar and combine until smooth.

3 Add egg and beat until completely combined. Add vanilla, flour, and cocoa powder. Stir to combine. Pour into a greased 8-ounce ramekin.

4 Pour water into Instant Pot® and add the trivet. Place ramekin on trivet.

5 Close the lid; turn the knob to Sealing.

6 Press Manual or Pressure Cook button and adjust time to 7 minutes.

7 When the timer beeps, immediately turn the knob from Sealing to Venting, then immediately remove the lid.

8 Carefully remove ramekin from the Instant Pot® and dab off any additional liquid that may have accumulated on top. Invert cake onto a plate and serve immediately.

PER SERVING

CALORIES: 941 | **FAT:** 52g | **PROTEIN:** 12g | **SODIUM:** 85mg
FIBER: 7g | **CARBOHYDRATES:** 116g | **SUGAR:** 99g

Small-Batch Cherry Cheesecake Bites

These deliciously smooth mini cheesecake bites are almost better than a full-sized cheesecake because each bite has an equal proportion of crust, cheesecake, sour cream, and topping!

- **Hands-On Time: 15 minutes**
- **Cook Time: 15 minutes**

Serves 1

Crust

4½ tablespoons graham cracker crumbs
2 tablespoons butter, melted
½ tablespoon all-purpose flour
⅛ teaspoon ground cinnamon
½ tablespoon sugar

Cheesecake Filling

8 ounces cream cheese, softened
5 tablespoons sugar
½ teaspoon vanilla extract
1 large egg, lightly beaten
1 tablespoon sour cream
1 cup water

Topping

2 tablespoons sour cream
6 tablespoons cherry pie filling

1 To make the Crust, in a medium bowl, combine all Crust ingredients. Add ½ tablespoon mixture into each cup of a silicone egg bites mold.

2 To make the Filling, in a separate medium bowl, mix together cream cheese and sugar until sugar is completely dissolved. Add vanilla, egg, and sour cream, and whisk until just combined. Do not overmix.

3 Pour filling evenly on top of crust. Place a paper towel on top of the mold, then cover tightly with foil.

4 Pour water into Instant Pot® and add the trivet. Place mold on trivet.

5 Close the lid; turn the knob to Sealing.

6 Press Manual or Pressure Cook button and adjust time to 5 minutes.

7 When the timer beeps, allow 10 minutes to naturally release the pressure, then remove the lid.

8 Carefully remove mold from the Instant Pot®. Remove foil and paper towel, and cool to room temperature 1–2 hours, then refrigerate overnight.

9 To serve, invert cheesecakes onto a plate or scoop them out with a large spoon and place on a plate.

10 Spread a thin layer of sour cream over each bite, and top with cherry pie filling. Serve.

PER SERVING

CALORIES: 1,614 | FAT: 101g | PROTEIN: 23g | SODIUM: 1,042mg
FIBER: 2g | CARBOHYDRATES: 128g | SUGAR: 83g

Key Lime Pie

This perfectly tart, smooth, sweet recipe tastes exactly like its classic big brother but in a perfect single portion.

- **Hands-On Time: 8 minutes**
- **Cook Time: 20 minutes**

Serves 1

Crust
¼ cup graham cracker crumbs
½ tablespoon sugar
1 tablespoon butter, melted
¹⁄₁₆ teaspoon ground cinnamon

Filling
1 large egg yolk
½ cup sweetened condensed milk
2 tablespoons lime juice
½ teaspoon lime zest
1 cup water

For Serving
2 tablespoons sweetened whipped cream
¼ teaspoon lime zest

1   In a medium bowl, mix together all Crust ingredients and press into an 8-ounce ramekin. Set aside.

2   In a separate medium bowl, mix together all Filling ingredients (except water) and pour over crust. Cover with foil.

3   Pour water into Instant Pot® and add the trivet. Place ramekin on trivet.

4   Close the lid; turn the knob to Sealing.

5   Press Manual or Pressure Cook button and adjust time to 10 minutes.

6   When the timer beeps, allow 10 minutes to naturally release the pressure, then remove the lid.

7   Let pie cool to room temperature, then refrigerate at least 6–8 hours or overnight.

8   Serve garnished with whipped cream and ¼ teaspoon lime zest.

PER SERVING

CALORIES: 633 | FAT: 27g | PROTEIN: 13g | SODIUM: 232mg
FIBER: 6g | CARBOHYDRATES: 89g | SUGAR: 69g

White Chocolate–Candy Cane Crème Brûlée

White chocolate and candy canes were just meant to be together! Add crème brûlée to the mix, and you've got yourself a delicious, festive holiday treat!

- **Hands-On Time: 10 minutes**
- **Cook Time: 26 minutes**

Serves 1

3 tablespoons white chocolate chips

½ cup heavy cream

2 large egg yolks

1 tablespoon sugar

1 cup water

1 tablespoon crushed candy cane, crushed into a fine powder

1 To a small bowl, add chocolate chips. In a small saucepan over medium-high heat, warm cream until steaming. Do not boil. Remove from heat and pour over chocolate chips and stir until melted.

2 In a separate small bowl, whisk egg yolks and sugar until light and smooth.

3 While whisking, slowly pour hot cream into egg yolks to temper the eggs. Whisk until completely combined.

4 Pour cream mixture through a fine-mesh strainer into an 8-ounce ramekin. Cover with foil.

5 Pour water into Instant Pot® and add the trivet. Place ramekin on trivet.

6 Close the lid; turn the knob to Sealing.

7 Press Manual or Pressure Cook button and adjust time to 16 minutes. Then press Pressure Level button and adjust to Low Pressure. If your Instant Pot® does not have a Low Pressure button, adjust the time to 12 minutes.

8 When the timer beeps, allow 10 minutes to naturally release the pressure, then remove the lid.

9 Carefully remove ramekin and place it on a cooling rack. Let cool to room temperature, then refrigerate 6–8 hours or overnight.

10 To serve, remove foil. Sprinkle peppermint candy evenly over the top of crème brûlée and shake to distribute it evenly. Using a kitchen torch, quickly torch candy in small circles until completely caramelized. Keep the torch moving to evenly melt candy.

11 Cool 1 minute, then serve immediately.

PER SERVING

CALORIES: 853 | **FAT:** 63g | **PROTEIN:** 10g | **SODIUM:** 98mg
FIBER: 0g | **CARBOHYDRATES:** 56g | **SUGAR:** 52g

Dairy-Free Coconut-Rice Pudding

You won't feel like you're missing or compromising anything with this incredibly coconutty, dairy-free rice pudding that uses cream of coconut and coconut milk. Cream of coconut is not the same thing as coconut cream, so do not substitute. Cream of coconut is a sweetened, syrupy ingredient that adds flavor and sweetness to the recipe.

- **Hands-On Time: 5 minutes**
- **Cook Time: 18 minutes**

Serves 1

½ cup uncooked long-grain
   white rice
1 cup water
⅟₁₆ teaspoon salt
2 tablespoons brown sugar
¼ cup cream of coconut
1 cup canned unsweetened
   full-fat coconut milk,
   divided
1 large egg
½ teaspoon vanilla extract
⅛ teaspoon ground cinnamon
½ tablespoon toasted
   shredded coconut

1 To the Instant Pot®, add rice, water, and salt. Close the lid; turn the knob to Sealing.

2 Press Manual or Pressure Cook button and adjust time to 3 minutes.

3 When the timer beeps, allow 10 minutes to naturally release the pressure, then remove the lid.

4 Fluff rice, then add brown sugar and cream of coconut. Stir to dissolve. Press Sauté button and adjust to Low. Add ½ cup coconut milk and bring to a low simmer, whisking constantly.

5 In a liquid measuring cup, measure remaining ½ cup coconut milk and whisk together with egg until completely combined.

6 While whisking, pour egg mixture into the pot until completely incorporated. Whisk about 5 minutes until thickened. Press Cancel button to turn off heat.

7 Stir in vanilla. Scoop into a bowl and serve with a sprinkle of cinnamon and toasted coconut.

PER SERVING

CALORIES: 1,229 | FAT: 59g | PROTEIN: 19g | SODIUM: 300mg
FIBER: 3g | CARBOHYDRATES: 154g | SUGAR: 68g

Creamy White Chocolate–Lemon Pie

This Creamy White Chocolate–Lemon Pie is an incredibly smooth, tart, and refreshing treat. Use one medium lemon for this recipe. If you prefer a more lemony pie, use up to double the amount of lemon juice.

- **Hands-On Time: 8 minutes**
- **Cook Time: 20 minutes**

Serves 1

Crust
¼ cup graham cracker crumbs
½ tablespoon sugar
1 tablespoon butter, melted

Filling
2 tablespoons white chocolate chips
¼ cup sweetened condensed milk
1 large egg yolk
2 tablespoons lemon juice
½ teaspoon lemon zest
1 cup water

1 To make Crust, in a small bowl, mix together all Crust ingredients and press into an 8-ounce ramekin. Set aside.

2 To make Filling, in a separate small microwave-safe bowl, microwave chocolate chips in 15-second intervals until melted.

3 Whisk in condensed milk, egg yolk, lemon juice, and lemon zest. Pour over the crust. Cover with foil.

4 Pour water into Instant Pot® and add the trivet. Place ramekin on trivet.

5 Close the lid; turn the knob to Sealing.

6 Press Manual or Pressure Cook button and adjust time to 10 minutes.

7 When the timer beeps, allow 10 minutes to naturally release the pressure, then remove the lid.

8 Let pie cool to room temperature, then refrigerate at least 6–8 hours or overnight, and then serve.

PER SERVING

CALORIES: 670 | FAT: 32g | PROTEIN: 12g | SODIUM: 227mg
FIBER: 1g | CARBOHYDRATES: 84g | SUGAR: 71g

US/Metric Conversion Chart

VOLUME CONVERSIONS

US Volume Measure	Metric Equivalent
⅛ teaspoon	0.5 milliliter
¼ teaspoon	1 milliliter
½ teaspoon	2 milliliters
1 teaspoon	5 milliliters
½ tablespoon	7 milliliters
1 tablespoon (3 teaspoons)	15 milliliters
2 tablespoons (1 fluid ounce)	30 milliliters
¼ cup (4 tablespoons)	60 milliliters
⅓ cup	90 milliliters
½ cup (4 fluid ounces)	125 milliliters
⅔ cup	160 milliliters
¾ cup (6 fluid ounces)	180 milliliters
1 cup (16 tablespoons)	250 milliliters
1 pint (2 cups)	500 milliliters
1 quart (4 cups)	1 liter (about)

WEIGHT CONVERSIONS

US Weight Measure	Metric Equivalent
½ ounce	15 grams
1 ounce	30 grams
2 ounces	60 grams
3 ounces	85 grams
¼ pound (4 ounces)	115 grams
½ pound (8 ounces)	225 grams
¾ pound (12 ounces)	340 grams
1 pound (16 ounces)	454 grams

OVEN TEMPERATURE CONVERSIONS

Degrees Fahrenheit	Degrees Celsius
200 degrees F	95 degrees C
250 degrees F	120 degrees C
275 degrees F	135 degrees C
300 degrees F	150 degrees C
325 degrees F	160 degrees C
350 degrees F	180 degrees C
375 degrees F	190 degrees C
400 degrees F	205 degrees C
425 degrees F	220 degrees C
450 degrees F	230 degrees C

BAKING PAN SIZES

American	Metric
8 x 1½ inch round baking pan	20 x 4 cm cake tin
9 x 1½ inch round baking pan	23 x 3.5 cm cake tin
11 x 7 x 1½ inch baking pan	28 x 18 x 4 cm baking tin
13 x 9 x 2 inch baking pan	30 x 20 x 5 cm baking tin
2 quart rectangular baking dish	30 x 20 x 3 cm baking tin
15 x 10 x 2 inch baking pan	30 x 25 x 2 cm baking tin (Swiss roll tin)
9 inch pie plate	22 x 4 or 23 x 4 cm pie plate
7 or 8 inch springform pan	18 or 20 cm springform or loose bottom cake tin
9 x 5 x 3 inch loaf pan	23 x 13 x 7 cm or 2 lb narrow loaf or pâté tin
1½ quart casserole	1.5 liter casserole
2 quart casserole	2 liter casserole

Index

Note: Page numbers in **bold** indicate category overview and recipe lists.